The History and Politics of UN Security Council Reform

'A very unique and concise monograph on the reform of the UN Security Council which analyses the main problem areas.'

Professor Reinhard Drifte, *University of Newcastle, UK*

'This is a scholarly treatment of a perennial theme in UN history. It is one where high principles and self-interest are intertwined in national policies, so as to produce an absorbing tale of usually fruitless initiatives for Security Council reform ... Anyone wanting to understand current debates over Security Council reform will find this historical study full of interest and insight. It is also a sobering reminder of how many proposals remain just that: proposals.'

Nicholas A. Sims, *Reader in International Relations, LSE, UK*

Using a political and historical approach, this new book delivers a penetrating analysis of the key issues surrounding UN Security Council reform.

This volume evaluates the historical development of efforts to reform the Security Council from 1946 until 2000. Bourantonis presents an overview of the current debates – emphasizing the potential for, and modalities of, adjustment in the post-Cold War era – through a systematic investigation of the various reform proposals and the attitudes of member states. He also provides an in-depth analysis of the 'sticking points' in the reform movement, including the right of veto, concerns about efficiency, legitimacy and representation, and the possibility of adding to the Security Council new members or new classes of membership.

This book will appeal to scholars of International Relations, and to all those interested in the UN and international organizations.

Dimitris Bourantonis is Assistant Professor of International Relations at the Athens University of Economics and Business.

Routledge advances in international relations and global politics

The History and Politics of UN Security Council Reform

Dimitris Bourantonis

Routledge
Taylor & Francis Group

LONDON AND NEW YORK

First published 2005
by Routledge
2 Park Square, Milton Park, Abingdon, Oxon OX14 4RN

Simultaneously published in the USA and Canada
by Routledge
270 Madison Ave, New York, NY 10016

Routledge is an imprint of the Taylor & Francis Group

Transferred to Digital Printing 2007

© 2005 Dimitris Bourantonis

Typeset in Sabon by Wearset Ltd, Boldon, Tyne and Wear

British Library Cataloguing in Publication Data
A catalogue record for this book is available from the British Library

Library of Congress Cataloging in Publication Data
A catalog record for this book has been requested

ISBN10: 0-415-30845-3 (hbk)
ISBN10: 0-415-45991-5 (pbk)

ISBN13: 978-0-415-30845-8 (hbk)
ISBN13: 978-0-415-45991-4 (pbk)

To Helen, Harris and Sofia

Contents

Acknowledgements

I am pleased to be able to offer my thanks to a number of people. I would like to express my appreciation to my colleague, Professor Euclid Tsakalotos, for his encouragement and valuable help throughout the various stages of my research. I am also very grateful to Dr Spyros Blavoukos and Stephen Key who read the whole text and helped me in clarifying a number of presentational points and improving the argument throughout. My special thanks are due, too, to the staffs of all the libraries in which I have worked, in particular for the assistance, patience and kind interest of the librarians and staffs at the London School of Economics and Political Science and the UN Information Offices in London and Athens, on whom I depended a great deal.

I have had very helpful comments on the original book proposal from a number of anonymous readers for Routledge. Heidi Bagtazo and Grace McInnes at Routledge were patient in the face of several changes to the delivery date caused by pressures of work. It goes without saying that responsibility for errors of fact and failings of judgement or interpretation lie solely and squarely with the author.

Abbreviations

CIS	Commonwealth of Independent States
ECOSOC	Economic and Social Council
EU	European Union
FAO	Food and Agriculture Organization
GAOR	General Assembly Official Records
IAEA	International Atomic Energy Agency
ICJ	International Court of Justice
NAM	Non-Aligned Movement
NATO	North Atlantic Treaty Organization
PKO	Peacekeeping operations
UN	United Nations
WHO	World Health Organization

Introduction

Three years ago three anonymous reviewers of a book proposal I had submitted to Routledge indicated the strong need for a book on Security Council reform. They claimed that a book-length treatment of the subject, which would address the historical process of Security Council reform, would be a welcome addition to the literature on the UN. They pointed out that although the reform of the Security Council has been an important part of UN history and politics, it has only occasionally been discussed by scholars and so far has not been the subject of a historical treatment. Whatever its achievement, this book is a positive response to that claim.

Indeed, the issue of Security Council reform has been the subject of many articles in academic journals[1] and of chapters in several edited volumes.[2] There are also scattered passages related to the issue in authored books about the Security Council[3] and in more general ones about the UN and international institutions.[4] Some of these works constituted policy papers, others were organized as conceptual discussions of the issues around Council reform or to inform us about the course of the negotiations at a particular stage, while still others appeared to be a mixture of these approaches. But none of them was written with the purpose of providing a historical account of the debates over Security Council reform since 1945.

The lack of historical study of this subject along with the fact that the issue of Security Council reform has been placed firmly near the top of the international agenda during the last two decades led to the publication of this book. It aims to take stock of and evaluate the historical development of efforts to reform the UN Security Council, from 1946, the year the most important political organ of the UN started to operate, until 2000. By offering a historical and political analysis of the reform movement, which has evolved throughout the life of the UN, this book will attempt to give insights into the difficulties and the complex issues surrounding Security Council reform. It also aims to give the reader a picture of the 'sticking points' in the reform movement, including the right of veto, possible changes in the Security Council's membership and its decision-making procedure and concerns about efficiency, legitimacy and representation.

For the purpose of this study, the concept of 'reform of the Security Council' refers to what has been described by Edward Luck as the attempts and/or acts of modifying the composition, the status and the voting powers of the members as well as the decision-making procedure of the Security Council.[5] Depending on the way reform is effected, one can make a distinction between *de jure* or *formal* reforms and *de facto* or *informal* reforms, the former referring to changes brought about through formal amendments or alterations in the text of the UN Charter and the latter changes without formal amendment of the UN Charter.

The scope of this study does not permit a detailed history of the Security Council reform movement. Such a history would require a series of books. Rather it will deal almost exclusively with the interplay between the five permanent members of the Council – which have assiduously resisted substantive changes in the structure of the Council – and some other key states or group of states that have from time to time articulated demands for reform. The focus will be on the most important phases of the debate on Council reform and on the discussion of the specific political developments and trends which produced them or followed them. In this context, only those proposals for reform that have influenced in one way or another the course of this debate will be examined.

The study is divided into five chapters, each referring to different chronological periods, which were chosen because of the changing scope of discussions about Security Council reform and the different approaches and attitudes of states to the issue in question. The basic point of departure for the work carried out in this study was the view that for a proper understanding of the historical process of reform, it was essential to grasp certain key political assumptions upon which the structure of the Security Council was founded in 1945 and to explain why its reform arose as a political necessity. Chapter 1 gives a brief historical background to the formation of the Security Council and focuses on its original structure. It also provides an explanation for the reasons reform became an integral part of the life of the Security Council and elaborates on the political difficulties encountered in the process of reform. Chapter 2 discusses the demands for reform raised during the Cold War with particular emphasis on the course of the negotiations that led to the 1965 expansion of the Security Council. Chapter 3 is an introduction to the post-Cold War debate on Council reform, illustrating why the case of Security Council reform gained momentum from the beginning of the 1990s. Major developments in international politics, such as the disintegration of the USSR and Yugoslavia, as well as early post-Cold War claims for changes in the structure of the Security Council are examined in this chapter. In addition, Chapter 3 provides a detailed account of the very interesting case of the Russian assumption of the old Soviet permanent seat, which constituted a *de facto* or informal reform of the Security Council. Chapter 4, which covers the period 1992–5, examines the various reform proposals, which were put forward by states at the negotiating table during the first post-Cold War round of debate that took place in the UN during this period. Chapter 5 carries the story forward by examining the ongoing debate on Council reform that took place in the period 1996–2000, with the point of departure being the so-called Razali Plan, the single most important and most coherent reform proposal ever tabled in the UN. The negative repercussions of this plan on the debate as well as the conflicting attitudes of the membership of the UN towards it are among the issues discussed in this chapter. Finally, the last chapter presents concluding remarks for the entire work which, it is hoped, are not merely of historical interest but provide a candid evaluation of the attitudes of the states towards the Security Council reform process and the nature of factors which have affected this process in both a positive and negative way.

1 The Security Council in 1945 and the quest for reform

The structure of the Security Council in 1945

Formation and function

When the UN Charter was being drafted, the end of the Second World War was still in sight, with easily discernible winners and losers. The intention was for the victorious states, which were the world's great powers at the time, to exercise global leadership with a view to managing or governing the international system. It was also perceived that the international order inaugurated in 1945 could be better sustained by a variety of international organizations. In the realm of global peace and security, this objective could be more effectively served by the creation of a universal organization through the institutional framework of which cooperation among the wartime allies would continue uninterrupted. Hence, the UN was set up with the Security Council as its dominant organ and beneath it the General Assembly and an array of other bodies dealing with specific issues, such as the ECOSOC, the Secretariat and the ICJ.

The overriding role of the Security Council reflected the strong desire of the founders of the UN to see it play an increasingly central role as the leading world forum for managing threats to the international order. To this end, the UN Charter recognized the Security Council as the organ with primary responsibility for international peace and security (Article 24), the maintenance of which would be realized in three ways. First, as outlined in Article 26 of the UN Charter, was the formulation of plans for the regulation of armaments. Second, international disputes or situations which were likely to endanger international peace and security would be settled in a peaceful manner following methods set out in Chapter VI of the Charter although 'decisions' of the Security Council would be framed as 'recommendations' and as such could have no legally binding effect on the members of the UN. Third, the Security Council was empowered to take enforcement action to deal with threats to the peace, breaches of the peace and acts of aggression. According to Chapter VII of the UN Charter, two distinct forms of enforcement measures were available to the executive organ of the UN: those stipulated in Article 40 and 41, not involving the use of armed force, and those described in Articles 42–45 involving military action by air, land and sea forces. The Security Council would have a monopoly on enforcement measures subject to two exceptions: first, the exercise of individual or collective self-defence (Article 51) and second, enforcement action taken by regional agencies authorized by the Security Council (Article 53). Chapter VII provided for a system of collective security (centred on the Security Council) for the enforcement of peace, which was more advanced than that of the League of Nations. Evidently, the clear conviction of the UN founders was that the UN, as an international security organization, should have 'teeth', that is increased power of enforcement against states violating peace. The experience of the League of Nations in the inter-war period had shown that international bodies which lack muscle and which are confined only to passing resolutions and issuing condemnations of aggressors are doomed to lose their creditability and legitimacy. Decisions of the Security Council acting under Chapter VII were framed as 'resolutions' in the sense that they were to be binding for all the member states regardless of their own vote or of their participation in the executive organ of the UN. The provision for the binding character of this type of Council decision was inserted into the Charter with a view to increasing the moral pressure on member states to implement the decisions of the governing body. Finally, there is a fourth function of the Security Council, that was not foreseen in the UN Charter but which developed later in practice: to authorize the launching of peacekeeping operations which were not seen as the pure military enforcement action envisaged under Chapter VII.

Apart from the primary functions bearing on international peace and security which were assigned to it, the Security Council was given the responsibility to carry out jointly with the General Assembly a number of secondary but important functions related to the internal operation of the UN. On certain important matters, the General Assembly cannot make a decision without a favourable recommendation from the Security Council. Such issues include the process of electing the Secretary-General (Article 97); the admission of new states to the UN (Article 4); the suspension of the exercise of the rights and privileges of membership (Article 5); and the expulsion of member states from the UN (Article 6).

The original composition

As originally conceived in the UN Charter, the Security Council was to be composed of 11 members of which five would be permanent members – the United States, the Soviet Union, Britain, France and China – all of whom would have the power of veto on substantive issues – and the other six would be non-permanent members. These non-permanent members were to be elected by a two-thirds majority of the General Assembly to serve for a two-year term. The UN Charter set two basic criteria to be applied in the election of the non-permanent members, namely, 'contribution of the members of the United Nations to the maintenance of international peace and security and to other purposes of the organization' and 'equitable geographical distribution' (Article 23).

The Security Council was structured in such a way as to embody the element of power (representation of power) and, at the same time, to reflect a proportional representation of the entire UN membership, consisting of large and small states.

Power representation and influence in the Security Council

The element of power was built into the Security Council's structure through the institutionalization of an inner group, consisting of the five most influential states, those that won the Second World War plus China. The idea of the major powers bearing great responsibility for the post-war order and, eventually, for the management of issues pertaining to international peace and security was uppermost in the minds of the founders of the UN. 'In their approach to the problem of building a security organization', they perceived that 'it might work with, rather than in opposition to, the realities of power'.[1] This was rooted in the assumption, derived from the realist theory, that the UN as an entity of sovereign states could work effectively only when individual states, particularly its most powerful members, conferred on it sufficient authority and competences. This led the founders of the UN to realize that if the great powers were to delegate authority and offer their political, military, technological and financial support to the Security Council, they should be given a privileged position in that organ. The privileged position of the great powers found recognition in the permanent status granted to them in the Security Council and the veto powers bestowed on them. Through this recognition, Roosevelt's idea of the continuation of the wartime alliance of the great powers acting as enforcers of post-war security was embedded in the structure of the UN and especially in the Security Council.

By conferring on the great powers of 1945 a superior status in the Security Council, the founders of the UN institutionalized an inner group of states within it which could exercise significant influence over Council decision-making.[2] This influence of the permanent five – which has been defined as 'the ability to determine outcomes' – could be either positive or negative.[3] The positive influence, based on the ability 'to get a resolution adopted', stemmed from their world status as great powers 'whose strength far outweighed all others'.[4] By way of persuasion, or through the offer of rewards or by what has been described by Holsti[5] and Russett[6] as 'implicit or explicit threats of punishment', the permanent seat occupants could exert a considerable degree of influence upon the other (non-permanent) members of the Council, thus impelling them to vote in favour of decisions which were useful or in the interests of the permanent five. As has already been stated, those which occupy non-permanent seats are usually small or medium-sized states dependent 'economically, militarily and politically upon the support of a great power'.[7] They could hardly cast a negative vote against the wishes of a great power. The negative influence of the great powers of 1945, which can be defined as their ability to prevent the Council from making decisions, which were deemed undesirable or detrimental to their interests, stemmed from the exceptional status they enjoyed in the Council, that is their permanency and the right of veto. The UN would not have been attractive to the great powers in 1945 had there not been adequate built-in safeguards to avert the risk of them being outvoted on issues touching upon their national interests. The possibility that one of them directly or indirectly, through allies, friends or proxies, might become involved in situations requiring international action, prompted the great powers to incorporate into the UN Charter the right of veto in effect giving them 'the legal and constitutional weapon with which they could defend their interests and position'.[8]

There was no doubt then that the permanent five could influence virtually all Council decisions bearing on international peace and security as well as important decisions taken by the General Assembly upon the recommendation of the Security Council. In addition to this, their ability to influence decisions on account of their great power status has been extended to other principal organs and agencies of the UN owing to the so-called *de facto* or unwritten privileges conferred on them (the so-called cascade effect of permanent membership).[9] Apart from the written privileges provided for in the UN Charter (their permanent status on the Council and their veto power), they have unwritten ones that have arisen from custom.[10] Council's permanent membership itself has guaranteed *de facto* permanent participation of the five in other principal UN organs, such as the ECOSOC and the ICJ. It has also resulted in the frequent appointment of nationals of the permanent five to key positions in the UN Secretariat. Due to their permanency, the five have ensured for themselves more frequent participation than the rest of the UN membership in ad hoc and subsidiary bodies of the General Assembly, such as the General Committee and in the executive bodies of several Specialized Agencies such as the IAEA, WHO and FAO (see Appendix 1).

The representation of UN membership, the effectiveness and efficiency of the Security Council

As already stated, the element of power was fully represented in the original structure of the Security Council. But the founders of the UN recognized that the element of power although necessary was not a sufficient condition to maintain for long the authority of the Council. They realized that the Security Council, when acting, as Article 24 of the UN Charter stipulates, on behalf of the membership as a whole, should be seen as representative of the entire UN membership. Otherwise its legitimacy and effectiveness would sooner or later be in jeopardy. Only if a majority of the original member states held the perception that they and their interests were represented in the composition of the Council, would they feel obliged to heed the body and comply with its decisions. Thus, the founders of the UN took care to make the Security Council somewhat representative of the UN membership. Indeed, the inclusion of six non-permanent members in the composition of the Security Council, along with the presence of the permanent five, made its composition reflect, on the basis of a more or less geographical balance, a microcosm of the UN membership. Apart from this, the small size of the body freed it from potential bureaucratic constraints and endowed it with efficiency, that is its ability to take, as stated in Article 24 of the UN Charter, 'prompt and effective action'. The Security Council's main function was to serve as an executive organ, able to take swift decisions at a moment's notice and to respond rapidly, whenever international peace and security were threatened (the efficiency argument).

Security Council: a case for adjustment

The need for reform

Despite the existence of an inner group of states with special privileges at its core, the Security Council, operating within the formal structure of a universal organization, purported to serve the cause of peace on a long-term basis. However, in order for the Security Council to survive for long, it needed to develop not only in accordance with the views of those who created it on the basis of the realities of 1945 but also in accordance with the transformations that had taken place in the real world since the birth of the institution in question. The Security Council could not remain a body sealed off from change in a world that was constantly changing. An international body that was not properly geared to the demands for change would either be relegated to the margins of international life or else it would simply die, as member states demanding a response to major world changes would turn away from it in frustration.

Indeed, during the years of the Cold War there were considerable changes on the international scene. As Morris put it 'Britain and France declined in relative power while other states grew in standing, most notably Germany and Japan but also a number of states in the south-eastern hemisphere'.[11] The culmination of the process of decolonization in the 1960s and the consequent admission to the UN of a large number of newly independent states, mostly from Africa but also from other parts of the developing world, brought about an explosive growth of UN membership and a significant alteration of its geopolitical synthesis. Even more significant international changes occurred with the end of the Cold War.

At that time the world witnessed the most dramatic shift in the distribution of power since 1945, as Russia, the successor of the Soviet Union, lost its empire and status as a global power. The demise of the Soviet Union drastically diminished the military might as well as the economic and political capabilities of one of the victors of the Second World War, thus putting into question its international influence. Today Russia (as well as China) can justify its seat as a permanent member of the Security Council mainly on account of population and territorial size, that is, on similar grounds to which some countries from the developing world, such as India, have based their claim to become permanent members. Furthermore, with the end of the Cold War, Britain and France saw their power further diminished. British and French claims to a permanent seat in 1945 by dint of their colonial possessions, or as a result of their experience in resolving post-colonial disputes,[12] could hardly be justified in the 1990s, as such colonial disputes had become a thing of the past. On the other hand, on the basis of their economic and political potential, Germany (especially after its unification) and Japan have made a dynamic comeback as major powers in the family of nations. Apart from shifts in power, the break up of the Soviet Union and Yugoslavia during the immediate post-Cold War period led to the creation of a host of new states, thus further expanding the membership of the UN.

Due to these dramatic changes, the Security Council as a political agency has come under pressure to adapt to the new situation. In fact, during the Cold War but more so during the post-Cold War era, the UN has been receptive to pressures from its member states to make the necessary adjustments to the Security Council's structure in order to retain its legitimacy and relevance in an evolving world.

The politics of reform

However, actual Security Council reform has proved to be a very difficult political task for a variety of reasons, the contest over reform turning out to be a struggle of member states to gain as much influence in the Security Council as possible. Changes in the composition of the Security Council or the voting rights or powers of its members might alter the degree of political influence which (permanent and non-permanent) members had at a given time and might stimulate an analogous trend within other organs either belonging to the UN (such as the ECOSOC) or to the Specialized Agencies of the UN. The most divergent interests, the most antagonistic ambitions and tendencies, the most contradictory views about Council reform came to the fore in the debate. The diversity of UN membership and, in consequence, the diversity of interests led states or groups of states to present and support different and sometimes contradictory reform plans and, as David Malone put it, 'to evaluate any reform proposal according to their own prospects of getting on [the Security Council] permanently or, alternatively, more frequently'.[13] A similar conclusion has been reached by Edward Luck, another expert on the UN. Attempting to draw lessons from the course of the debate on Council reform he concluded that for member states what really mattered in assessing any reform initiative was 'who was putting forward the proposal, and what each group might be expected to gain or lose from it'.[14] The fact that 'each state or group of states looked to its own national advantage'[15] when it was called to discuss Council reform rendered the search for consensus on the basic issues of reform a highly complex task.

In attempting to reform the Security Council, member states faced the difficulty of maintaining a fragile balance between representation, legitimacy and efficiency.[16] On the one hand, an increase in the membership of the Security Council would make this body more representative and democratic and therefore more legitimized. On the other hand, a broad expansion of the Security Council's membership would inevitably create a top-heavy and cumbersome body that would have great difficulty in acting swiftly and effectively. In all likelihood, such an expansion would lead to a loss of efficiency similar to that experienced by the League of Nations. Due to several increases in membership of the Council of the League, the Council became, as Edward Carr observed, more representative, but 'lost much of its effectiveness as a political instrument'. Carr was right to indicate that the principle of representation is an abstract one. As he rightly underlined 'reality was sacrificed to an abstract principle [i.e. that of representation]'.[17] Indeed, it could be claimed that the composition of the executive bodies of international organizations should not be determined solely on the basis of the abstract principle of representation. Member states cannot easily find an answer to the question of how many states (and under what criteria) should be represented in the Security Council in order to make it reflect the UN membership. But one thing is certain: so long as demands for reforming the Security Council are persistently raised but not dealt with in a satisfactory manner, the legitimacy of the Security Council will continue to be in question.

Finally, and this is crucial, one cannot ignore the fact that progress towards reforming the Security Council will be made only if the member states can overcome the constitutional difficulty of amending the UN Charter. Any change in the Council's membership or in the voting power of its members requires the unanimous consent of the permanent five. The main drafters of the Charter, the United States, Britain and the Soviet Union, were not only responsible for the creation of the Security Council's structure but also for the insertion of a procedure for amendment of the UN Charter which requires the consent of the permanent five to any amendment. Article 108 of the UN Charter stipulates that

> amendments to the present Charter shall come into force for all members of the United Nations when they have been adopted by a vote of two-thirds of [all] the members of the General Assembly and

ratified in accordance with their respective constitutional processes by two-thirds of the members of the United Nations, including all the permanent members of the Security Council.

In effect, Article 108 of the UN Charter inserted a blocking element in the reform process in the sense that power would be in the hands of the five permanent members of the Council to accept or reject amendments and they would be unlikely to do anything which might jeopardize their privileged position. If the Security Council was really to reflect the international distribution of power at any given time, it would have entailed the relegation of some from the select group as well as the appointment of others. It is difficult to imagine one of the permanent five accepting its relegation from the select club. The elevation of some states to permanent membership without necessarily displacing any of the current permanent five would imply the relative diminution of the political influence of the current permanent members. Would the permanent five accept this? Would they accept sharing their privileged position in the Security Council and a redistribution of the so called 'fringe' benefits enjoyed by them by virtue of their permanency (such as permanent representation in other UN bodies, or very frequent participation in the executive Councils of various specialized agencies) with some other states? Would they accept merely an expansion of the non-permanent seats given that such an expansion would bring about an increase in the size of the Council, thus inevitably raising the issue of voting threshold? Since the Council operates under majority rule, any enlargement would necessitate a change in the number of votes required for decisions. This might reduce the capacity of the permanent five to exercise their 'positive influence' in the Security Council. Still worse, a broad expansion of the number of non-permanent members would be likely to give them power, if they could stick together as a bloc, to exercise in certain cases 'negative influence', a so-called sixth veto.

2 Demands for reform in the Cold War era

The early years (1946–54)

During the early life of the UN there was no change in the composition or the voting powers of the permanent or non-permanent members of the Security Council, a consequence of the fact that the number of member states of the UN changed little during the first nine years of its life. Indeed, during the period 1946–54, 31 states had applied for admission for UN membership, but only nine of them were admitted owing to the East–West conflict. As the membership issue became entangled in the politics of the Cold War, each camp made use of the veto to block candidates supported by the other. Many qualified states were kept out for years solely because the use of the veto prevented the Security Council from making favourable recommendations to the General Assembly (Article 4 of the UN Charter). As a result, no demands for Council reform were articulated by member states, which perceived the composition of the Security Council to be more or less representative of the UN.

The only change of note during the early life of the Security Council concerned the practice of voluntary abstention by a permanent member in a vote on matters of substance. Here it was accepted that such an abstention would not be interpreted as a negative vote. Article 27 (3), as it was originally formulated in the UN Charter, required, in substantive matters, an affirmative vote of seven members [out of eleven] of the Council, 'including the concurring votes of the [five] permanent members'. Since the earliest days of the UN, however, the permanent members, contrary to understandings reached at San Francisco[1] as to the meaning of Article 27 (3), had adhered to the view that voluntary abstention on their part from voting in the Security Council was not tantamount to a veto. Their argument was that 'a permanent member which has the opportunity to exercise its right of veto but chooses to refrain from exercising it should not be obliged to have its abstention [or absence from voting] counted as a negative vote'.[2] The permanent members accepted the practice of the Security Council in not treating the abstention of a permanent member as a negative vote as a means to smooth away the difficulties that would arise from the rigid application of the veto, as per Article 27 (3). This practice proved to be of considerable political importance because during the Cold War it led to the adoption of numerous decisions which otherwise would not have been taken with one or more permanent members abstaining. As Liang pointed out, 'had the abstentions been considered as negative votes, the Security Council would have adopted very few substantive decisions' in its more than ten years' history.[3]

The membership of the Security Council in its early years was a reflection of the principal elements of power in the UN on the one hand and the major regional groups of states on the other. During this period the distribution of the non-permanent seats on the Security Council followed, more or less, the lines of the gentlemen's agreement reached informally by the five permanent members of the Council in 1946. As Bailey remarked, the precise content of the gentlemen's agreement was never published, but its existence was acknowledged by the permanent five. The Soviet Union, for instance, explicitly stated in the UN that under the terms of the gentlemen's agreement, the permanent members were committed to support the election of the non-permanent seats in accordance with a fixed formula of regional distribution. As the Soviets asserted, the permanent five

> undertook to support the election to the Council of candidates nominated by the countries of the five main regions of the world. In accordance with that plan it was agreed that in the election of non-permanent members support would be given to two countries from the Latin-American region ... while one seat would be allotted to the British Commonwealth, one to the Middle East, one to Western Europe, and one to Eastern Europe.[4]

However, the pattern of geographical allocation of the elective (non-permanent) seats left the African and Asian states dissatisfied. They felt resentment against the sponsoring powers of the agreement. Some of them, like India, never recognized the validity of this agreement and felt bound to challenge it. As the Indian representative in the UN asserted, the gentlemen's agreement, which was used as guidance for the distribution of Council seats, was never endorsed by the General Assembly. It had been reached secretly by the permanent five and as such it could not bind the membership of this organ.[5]

While it is true that the regions of Africa and Asia were not given non-permanent representation on the Security Council, it is not entirely accurate to say that states from these two regions were very unfairly dealt with by the sponsoring powers. Under the gentlemen's agreement, a representative number of African and Asian states members of the UN had a fair chance to stand for election via the British Commonwealth and the Middle East seats. As a writer on the UN rightly stressed, 'only twelve of the UN's fifty-one original members came from Asia or Africa, and of these China

was a permanent member of the Council, India was in the Commonwealth, and seven states were in the Middle East'. Only Ethiopia and
Liberia had not been given the opportunity to be elected to non-permanent
seats by the gentlemen's agreement.[6]

The argument that the gentlemen's agreement constituted to some
degree a satisfactory arrangement for the non-permanent representation of
the African and Asian states on the Security Council proved to be correct
in practice. India was elected by the General Assembly to the Security
Council's non-permanent membership in 1946 for a one-year term as well
as in the period 1950–1. Egypt and Middle East states that belonged to the
Afro-Asian group were also elected to serve as non-permanent members.
Pakistan, which was admitted in the UN in 1947, was elected to fill the
vacancy for the British Commonwealth for the period 1952–3. Needless to
say, this arrangement suited all members except those which belonged to
Eastern Europe who, from 1950, had seen their right to occupy their share
of seats as non-permanent members of the Security Council being under-
mined as members of the General Assembly chose to circumvent the gen-
tleman's agreement using the Eastern European seat to elect non-Eastern
European states. This situation continued for more than a decade. Thus,
the non-permanent seat that should have been occupied, under the terms
of the 1946 Agreement, by an Eastern European state was filled, in succession, by Yugoslavia for the 1950–1 term and for 1956 (one year), Greece
for 1952–3 and Turkey for 1954–5. Yugoslavia could not be counted as
belonging to the Soviet bloc because it had broken ties with Moscow and
appeared unwilling to represent Eastern European views. Neither Greece
nor Turkey belonged to the Eastern bloc but were politically allied with
the Western powers and had become members of NATO. Growing pressure for African and Asian representation led the General Assembly to fill
the Eastern European seat by the Philippines for 1956 (one year), by Japan
(1958–9), by Poland and Liberia for 1960–1 (each one for one year), by
Romania and the Philippines for the 1962–3 term.[7]

The rise of demands for an expansion of the Security Council (1955–6)

The UN had barely passed its tenth birthday before its members started to
call for changes in the composition of the Security Council. In 1955, the
United States and the Soviet Union agreed not to block any future applications for membership in the UN, an agreement which was hailed as 'an
event second only to the foundation of the United Nations itself'.[8] The difficulty that had impeded the admission of new states was removed and the
drive in favour of universality of UN membership gained momentum. This
led to a substantial increase in the membership of the UN in the following
years. Sixteen new members were admitted in 1955, four in 1956, six in
1957, and 20 in the period between 1957 and 1960.[9] By 1960, UN mem-

bership had risen to 99 and the ratio of elective seats on the Council to the total membership of the UN had fallen dramatically. In the period 1961–3 this ratio fell further because 12 new states joined the ranks of UN membership, which rose to 113. Except for the membership of the Latin American group, which remained constant, and the membership of the Commonwealth group, which changed little, there was a significant increase in the membership of the Western and Eastern European groups. But, more importantly, there was a dramatic increase in the number of African and Asian members, which by 1963 constituted more than half the UN's membership and now aspired to be fairly represented on the Security Council.[10]

The large influx of new states brought with it an intensification in the competition for non-permanent seats on the Security Council, it being argued that a fair 'equitable geographical distribution' of the non-permanent seats in the Security Council should be sought. The gentlemen's agreement of 1946, on the basis of which the non-permanent seats had been so far distributed, had to a large extent become obsolete. It had to be superseded by another agreement that would reallocate the seats taking into account the new geographical distribution of the UN's membership. For many medium and smaller states this reallocation should come after an agreement for an expansion of the composition of the Security Council. Undoubtedly, the huge increase in the number of member states had brought about pressures, especially from the African and Asian states, for a reconsideration of the original composition of the Security Council.

The question of enlarging the Security Council was first raised following the admission of 16 new states in 1955. At the 11th session of the General Assembly, 16 Latin American states[11] and Spain jointly took the initiative to propose that the General Assembly immediately consider amending the UN Charter so as to increase the number of non-permanent members of the Security Council and the majority required for its decisions. They introduced a draft resolution by which the General Assembly was called upon to adopt amendments to Article 23 and 27 of the UN Charter. Their proposal called for an increase of the non-permanent seats from six to eight (and thereby an increase in the membership of the Security Council from 11 to 13) and a change in the number of votes required for Security Council decisions from seven to eight.[12] The Latin American states also proposed an enlargement of the 16-member ECOSOC in order to facilitate the participation of new states in that organ and an amendment to the Statute of the ICJ in order to increase the number of judges in the Court.

It was surprising, perhaps, that those which took the leadership in proposing an expansion of the non-permanent membership of the Council were not the African or Asian states but those belonging to the Latin American group. They had good reasons to do so. Shortly after the first wave of admissions of new states to the UN in 1955, several member states, including some permanent members, had expressed the view that there was no need for Council expansion and that the 'unfairness' of the 1946 agreement could be corrected by the redistribution of the six elective seats among the overrepresented geographical regions. A sudden fear came over the Latin American states that an arrangement for the redistribution of the existing elective seats might involve taking away a non-permanent seat from them. In other words, it might cost their geographical region the loss of one out of the two elective seats originally allotted to it by the 1946 agreement. Thus, the Latin American states acted with haste to table their proposal at the General Assembly in order to shift the discussion in the UN away from the issue of redistribution of the existing seats and raise instead the issue of Council expansion. They believed that their proposal could win support among the member states for a variety of reasons. It would be well received by the permanent members who would see little or no disadvantage to their national interests in accepting a very modest increase in Council's membership. Adding only two elective seats would raise no problem about permanent membership, thus leaving the status and the privileges of the permanent five untouched. The proposal sought to disturb as little as possible the basic structure, the political balance and the voting requirements of the Security Council. This led the sponsors of the proposal to believe that the permanent five would consider it seriously. Second, it was expected that the reform proposal would appeal to many small and middle-sized states, the prime beneficiaries of the Spanish proposal being the African and Asian states which had been solidly in the forefront of demanding Security Council enlargement along lines suggested by the Latin American states.

Expansion becomes hostage of inter-issue bargaining (1957–65)

In putting forward their reform proposal, the Latin American states never thought that the question of the expansion of the Council would be intimately intertwined with the politics of Chinese representation in the UN.[13] The enlargement of the Security Council could not be achieved except by an amendment of the UN Charter, which could only occur with the approval of all five permanent members. This, the Soviet Union intimated, could not be obtained until the People's Republic of China had assumed its rightful place in the UN. The Soviets warned that they would never ratify amendments to the UN Charter without the participation of communist China as a full member of the UN and a permanent member of the Security Council. Having proclaimed themselves custodians of the UN Charter, they asserted that 'an amendment of the Charter could not be agreed upon in the absence of representatives of the People's Republic of China and could not enter into force without ratification by that Government'.[14]

The settlement of the question of Chinese representation in the UN organs was, however, only one of the two conditions set out by the Soviet

Union and the Eastern European states in order to enter into a discussion with the rest of the UN membership about the expansion of the Security Council. The other condition had to do with the highly irregular situation that existed with regard to the representation of the Eastern European states in the Security Council. For a long time Eastern Europe had not in practice had the measure of representation which it was entitled to receive under the terms of the 1946 gentlemen's agreement. The Soviet Union and its allies accordingly notified the other member states that they would refuse to discuss proposals for Council expansion which would not eliminate the practice of snatching seats from the group of Eastern European states (as happened in 1952–3 and 1953–4 when Greece and Turkey respectively occupied the East European seat). As Schwelb, a writer on the UN, wrote, the Soviets and their allies made clear that they were not going to give 'their consent to the proposed enlargement of the Security Council without some guarantee in writing that they [i.e. the Eastern bloc countries] would not be deprived of representation on the Council'.[15]

In fact, such an explicit guarantee was missing from the Latin American proposal and so, with a view to satisfying the Soviet Union and the Eastern European states, the original proposal was improved by the incorporation into it of an explicit and clear pattern of distribution of the non-permanent (elective) seats. This pattern purported to allocate two seats to Latin America, two seats to Asia and Africa, one seat to the Commonwealth of Nations, two seats to Western and Southern Europe and one seat to Eastern Europe.

The pattern of geographical distribution suggested by the Latin American states gave some satisfaction to the Eastern European states and principally to the Soviet Union which desired to have one of its own allies regularly on the Security Council. It also pleased the older Commonwealth states, which were primarily concerned with retaining the separate Commonwealth seat while supporting a modest increase in total seats. It was also welcomed by the West Europeans, who would now be allotted two non-permanent seats instead of one and, certainly, by the Afro-Asian states, which would at last assume their rightful place among the other geographical groups.

Despite all this, no action was taken on the Latin American proposal at the 11th session of the General Assembly (1956), owing to the rigid attitude of the Soviet Union and its allies, all of which insisted that no positive solution to the issue of Council expansion was possible until the People's Republic of China was fully represented in the UN.[16] The uncompromising attitude of the Soviet Union left no prospect for any agreement on expansion at the time and led the General Assembly to postpone consideration of the issue. For the same reason the General Assembly decided to put off discussion of the issue in question at its 12th (1957), 13th (1958) and 14th (1959) sessions.[17]

Undoubtedly, the question of the representation of China turned out to be of crucial importance for the expansion of the Security Council, proving to be the biggest stumbling block in the talks about expansion for seven years until the 18th session of the General Assembly in 1963. This was a period at the height of the Cold War when relations between the Soviet Union and the United States were visibly strained, a situation which was reflected in all activities of the UN. Hence, the issue of Council expansion became intertwined with the problems of great power relations, which had, by this time, converted the UN into a divided world. The Soviet Union and its allies (Bulgaria, Belorussia, Czechoslovakia, Hungary, Poland, Romania and the Ukraine) in effect made an expansion of the Council conditional upon the solution of the question of Chinese representation, using all those states which were campaigning for Council expansion, and especially the Afro-Asian states, as a lever for bringing pressure to bear upon the United States. The Soviet Union believed that the United States could not afford to have it appear to other member states that the case for Council expansion was impeded by its negative stance on the Chinese issue. In such a case it would appear publicly that in reality the policy of the Soviet Union was all for Council expansion and if it did not come about it was not its fault but the fault of the United States. The state-ment of the Soviet representative to the UN is very revealing about the real intentions of Moscow: 'everyone knew that international problems could not be solved without the participation of the People's Republic of China and that it was not the USSR but the western powers that were responsible for the legitimate indignation of the African and Asian countries'.[18]

Moscow apparently believed that time was on its side and for several years deliberately employed the tactic of connecting the question of Chinese representation with the issue of Council expansion. From a short-term perspective, this tactic created a sense of frustration among those states which were ardent supporters of Council expansion because it turned out to be non-negotiable for the time being. From a long-term perspective, it turned out to be self-defeating. At the end of the day the Soviets realized that they had come out of the debate badly and this made them review their policy towards Council expansion.

The move of the Soviet Union to tie the question of Council expansion to the issue of seating communist China took every member state in the UN by surprise, most of them believing that such a link would complicate rather than promote a solution to the problem of the enlargement of the Council's membership. While a large number of them were sympathetic to an early seating of Peking in the UN, the majority of them refused to see the admission of communist China as the most pressing issue. They were of the view that if they accepted giving priority to the settlement of the Chinese issue over the issue of Council expansion, the latter would in all probability be doomed to remain pending indefinitely. Among those that shared this belief were, of course, the members of the Afro-Asian group which had become by far the strongest numerical force in the UN with the admission of new states in 1960.[19] It was also shared by the Latin American states, which still feared that a further delay in reaching a decision on Council expansion might force the Afro-Asian states to ask for a redistribution of the existing seats on the Council. In such a case, the number of seats assigned to Latin American states might be reduced in order to satisfy the ambitions of the Afro-Asian states. The same fear arose among the Western European states. The existing distribution of the permanent seats was, in fact, favourable to Western Europe, which was represented in the club of permanent members by two states (Britain and France). The risk was that a redistribution of the non-permanent seats might force them to yield their single non-permanent seat.

The Afro-Asian and Latin American states realized that unless they made a move soon, they would be in a hopelessly weak position to promote Council expansion in the years to come. They had to take initiatives in order to (i) keep the member states entrenched in the debate on Council expansion rather than on the Chinese issue and (ii) exert pressure upon the Soviet Union to shift its ground. Thus, in 1960, 39 of them tabled a draft resolution in the Special Political Committee of the General Assembly, which contained a proposal for Council expansion akin to that which the Latin American group had submitted in 1956. They proposed an increase of the number of non-permanent members of the Security Council from six to eight and of the total size of the Council from 11 to 13.[20] The proposal was, however, doomed to failure. The draft resolution did not receive the necessary number of votes to effect a Charter amendment. Some states, convinced that, as a consequence of the Soviet threat not to ratify the UN Charter amendment, it would be meaningless to pass such a resolution, did not vote for it.[21]

The Soviet Union not only stood pat during the debate in the Special Political Committee, but it appeared to have a new surprise in store for the member states. Apart from the settlement of the Chinese issue, they set out a new condition for amending the Charter. They, along with the other members of the Eastern bloc, made it clear that they would not accept amendments to the Charter unless the structure of the UN Secretariat, including of course the office of the Secretary-General, was so modified as to reflect an equal representation of only three groups: the Eastern, the Western and the non-aligned states (neutralists).[22] This modification, the Soviet Union claimed, would be necessary in order to bring the structure of the Secretariat into harmony with the division of the world into the above-mentioned three groups of states.

The claim of the Soviet Union for equal tripartite representation of the three groups in the UN Secretariat was inconsistent with its insistence on the settlement of the Chinese question prior to Council expansion and was made 'at a time when the Soviet Union conducted an energetic campaign for a fundamental rebuilding of the United Nations, its representative bodies and its Secretariat'.[23] The restructuring of the UN, according to the

Soviet viewpoint, had to be made on the basis of the principle of equal representation between the three groups of states in the UN organs, which would in effect increase the representation of the Eastern group in the institutions of the world organization.

The Soviet attack on the UN Secretariat was specifically directed against the person of the Secretary-General. The Soviet demand for an equal tripartite representation came at a time when their diplomatic attack on the then Secretary-General Dag Hammarskjold had been stepped up. Hammarskjold, they believed, exercised more than merely administrative powers. Moscow was infuriated by the way he performed his duties, regarding him as partial, favouring Western policies in the UN. Within the context of the principle of equal tripartite representation, the Soviets developed their so-called troika proposal. The central idea on which the troika concept was based was to change the office of a single Secretary-General and replace it by a new collective executive. This would consist of three persons (administrators), each one representative of one of the three groups of states – the Eastern, the Western and the non-aligned – on the basis of equality. Each of them, and consequently each of the groups of states, would possess a right to exercise a veto over any action of the collective executive.

A new political force comes in on the talks

The attitude of the Soviet bloc angered, most of all, the Afro-Asian states which were constantly agitating for changes in the composition of the Security Council. These states convened, for the first time since the Bandung conference of 1955, a summit in Belgrade in September 1961, a conference that marked the genesis of the NAM. The formation of the Movement reflected the will of its members to create and maintain a cohesive and well organized coalition of states aimed at playing a major regulatory role in the international arena, including the UN, through collective and well orchestrated actions. As Jackson wrote, the common purpose of these states was the formulation of policies 'independent of the superpowers or associated blocs, then polarized by the Cold War'.[24] The Movement was destined to be 'an alternative to these divisions, not as a bloc in its own right'.[25] For these purposes the Movement began to organize from time to time conferences at the highest political level in order to generate and maintain internal loyalties among its members and to formulate common policies and adopt common attitudes with regard to the most pressing issues on the international agenda. Sponsoring draft resolutions, and in approaching the UN generally, they based their position primarily on the political guidelines of their conferences. The membership of the Movement, which originally consisted of 24 Afro-Asian states plus Yugoslavia, was widely expanded in the following years to include the overwhelming majority of the Afro-Asian states and a large number of states from Latin America and the Caribbean. By the New Delhi summit in 1983, 99 states were full members of the NAM.

The structure of the UN was one of the six major issues discussed by the non-aligned states at the Belgrade summit.[26] During the summit the non-aligned states took the Soviet Union's proposal for the tripartite control of the UN as an attempt to prevent the non-aligned states from widening their political influence on it. The members of the NAM anxiously awaited an increase in their role in the various organs of the UN as a consequence of their rapidly growing number. By maximizing their influence in the UN, they would be in a position to assume a major role in world affairs and at the same time play a highly influential role in rebuilding the UN, step by step, including the Security Council and the institution of Secretary-Generalship. Seemingly, the Soviet pattern of tripartite representation appeared to offer the non-aligned states more participation in the UN Secretariat. But in reality, it would neutralize their potential of emerging as a group which, based on its steadily growing numerical strength, could bring about changes in the UN as a whole. Furthermore, they took the Soviet proposal as an attempt to weaken the UN, an institution upon which they wanted to capitalize in order to promote their own interests. As Haile Selassie, Emperor of Ethiopia, warned during the Belgrade conference: 'anyone who acts deliberately and with calculation to the injury of the UN, to weaken it or endanger its existence as an effective and energetic institution, is the enemy of us'.[27] Thus, the non-aligned states rejected the Soviet pattern of troika control of the Secretariat.

There was also agreement among the members of the NAM during the Belgrade summit that, contrary to what the Soviet Union alleged, the expansion of the membership of the Security Council and the restoration of communist China's rights in the UN are two different and unconnected questions. This was reflected in the final Declaration of the 1961 summit of the NAM.[28] Paragraph 24 of this declaration stipulated that

> the participating countries consider it essential that the General Assembly of the UN should ... find a solution to the question of expanding the membership of the Security Council and of the Economic and Social Council in order to bring the composition and work of these two important organs of the United Nations into harmony with the needs of the Organization and with the expanded membership of the United Nations.

By refusing to recognize a connection between the two issues, the members of the NAM wanted to deliver an unequivocal message to the Soviet Union: it had to lift its objections to Council enlargement and cease using the Afro-Asian states as a lever for exercising pressure on the United States for a settlement of the Chinese issue. Apart from their desire to see the Security Council enlarged in order to assume their places in it, the

Afro-Asian members of the NAM had another compelling reason to deny the Soviet proposal to connect the two questions. They were divided over whether the Chinese issue should be promptly solved or its settlement should be postponed for the future. This was a consequence of the rift that had started between China and India in 1959 due to Chinese incursions into Indian territory. Several of them felt ill-disposed towards the immediate recognition of China's rights in the UN, as was evidenced in the language of paragraph 26 of the Final Declaration of the Belgrade summit where it was made clear that some NAM members were not prepared to offer recognition to the People's Republic:

> those of the participating states in the conference *who recognize the Government of the People's Republic of China* recommend that the General Assembly in its forthcoming session should accept the representatives of the Government of the People's Republic of China as the only legitimate representative of that country in the United Nations.[29] (emphasis added)

The dissension that existed among the members of NAM with regard to the settlement of the Chinese issue was further manifested in the General Assembly in 1961 where the votes of the Afro-Asian group were divided, with 26 in favour of China's admission, 14 against and six abstentions.

The 1963 breakthrough

The attitude of the non-aligned states eventually led the Soviet Union to withdraw its proposal for tripartite representation in the UN organs. However, throughout the period 1962–3 the Soviet Union continued to link the issue of Council expansion with the Chinese question and was greatly vexed to see that there was now general discontent among the member states with its attitude. Indeed, a large number of Latin American and European states, including Italy, the Netherlands, Belgium and Britain, and states like Australia, Canada and Japan were noticeably displeased with the Soviet attitude. Complaints against the Soviet stance were made also by the United States which, by expressing its support for a limited expansion of the Council, had managed to make its attitude towards Council enlargement look moderate in contrast to the hard-line attitude of the Soviet Union.

In 1963, two groups of states, which had vested interests in seeking Council expansion, submitted to the Special Political Committee of the General Assembly two different draft resolutions containing Charter amendments. On 10 December 1963, 21 Latin American states resubmitted their draft resolution calling for the Charter to be amended to increase the membership of the Council from 11 to 13 by the addition of two non-permanent seats.[30] This was followed, on 13 December, by a draft resolution submitted by 37 Afro-Asian states seeking to increase the membership of the Council to 15 by the addition of four non-permanent seats. According to the second draft resolution, the number of non-permanent members would be increased from six to ten, of whom five would be drawn from African and Asian states (three would be allocated to Africa and two to Asia), two from Latin America and Caribbean states, two from Western Europe and others and one from Eastern European states.[31] After a series of consultations among the delegations of the Latin American states and the Afro-Asian states, the former agreed to incorporate in their draft resolution the figures of the Afro-Asian draft.[32] By sponsoring one single draft resolution calling for a fifteen – instead of a thirteen – member Security Council, the Latin American states and the African and Asian states intended to put more pressure on members of the UN, and especially on the Soviet Union, to acquiesce in the enlargement of the Council. The draft resolution was also 'a searching proposal' in the sense that it was sponsored for the purpose of testing the sincerity of the Western powers, and especially of the United States, Britain and France, which for several years had professed themselves in favour of an enlargement of the Council's non-permanent membership.

The debate on the draft resolution that took place in the Special Political Committee of the General Assembly in December 1963 proved to be more acrimonious than ever before. The three Western permanent members expressed opposition to the draft resolution. The representative of the United States stated that it 'was authorized to vote in favour only of amendments to the Charter providing for a thirteen-member Security Council' and that 'it had no authority to support any other proposals'.[33] A similar view was expressed by Britain, which had one more reason to vote against the draft resolution, if it were put to a vote, as it attached particular importance to the retention of Commonwealth seats in the enlarged Council. These were the ones that would be affected the most by the draft resolution which provided for a pattern of distribution of non-permanent seats which would, in effect, entirely remove formal Commonwealth representation from the elective seats of the Security Council. Of the three Western permanent members, France was the only one not to explain its negative attitude toward the draft resolution. But it shared the view expressed by the other two powers, that the Special Political Committee and the General Assembly should defer action on the question of Council expansion until at least the following year.[34]

Despite all this, it was then clear that for the United States, Britain and France the question was no longer whether to increase the number of non-permanent seats, but by how much. The fact that the three powers approached the issue of Council expansion with sympathy brought satisfaction to the sponsors of the draft resolution and especially to the Afro-Asian states. As a result, they chose to follow a tactical position not to become embroiled in a dispute with the three Western powers. Instead, all their acrimony was directed against the Soviet Union, which continued maintaining its negative attitude towards an amendment of the UN Charter to expand the Security Council so long as communist China of 600 million people was denied the right to its seat in the UN. As the debate in the Special Political Committee continued, the African states appeared to become more assertive that ever. Acting in conformity with what had been agreed at the Addis Ababa Conference[35] of African heads of state in May 1963, they condemned the status quo attitude of the Soviets and questioned 'the seriousness of the Soviet threat to veto the contemplated amendments to the Charter'.[36]

In an attempt to defend its position, the Soviet Union went so far as to say that the government of communist China at this stage favoured, not Council expansion through an amendment of the UN Charter, but the redistribution of the existing six non-permanent seats. In support of its statement about China's attitude, the Soviet Union told the member states that it had approached the Chinese government and requested it to clarify its position on the question under discussion. The Soviets stated in the Special Political Committee that their government had received an official reply from the government of China on 12 December 1963 that contained the following statement: 'We do not approve of the solving of this problem [i.e. the problem of representation of the Afro-Asian states in the Security Council] through an increase in the membership of United Nations organs; we favor its solution through equitable distribution of the existing seats in those organs [i.e. the Security Council and the Economic and Social Council]'.[37] The Chinese Government was also reported by the Soviets to have declared in its statement of 12 December that a redistribution of existing seats in the Security Council was 'much simpler and easier to operate in existing conditions' than an enlargement which would entail a UN Charter amendment. The latter 'involves questions which are highly complicated and are connected with extremely complicated procedures'.[38] The Soviets gave the member states to understand that what they gathered from this statement was the willingness of the Chinese Government to see the question of Council expansion linked with that of recognizing Peking's legitimate rights in the UN.

The Soviet allegations called forth numerous comments from member states and triggered a big political row initially in the Special Political Committee and subsequently in the plenary meeting of the General Assembly. The interest switched to the Chinese stand. Albania, which 'was well known in recent years to have acted as spokesman for mainland China', reacted promptly to the Soviet allegations about the Chinese stand. Its representative stated that he did not think 'it fair that a member [i.e. the Soviet Union] should invoke the People's Republic of China to justify its own position'.[39] African and Asian states found it difficult to believe what the delegates of the Soviet Union insisted were the true preferences of the People's Republic of China. The Afro-Asian states knew well that communist China needed their support in its diplomatic struggle to win its seat in the UN and in the Security Council. Apart from that, the Soviet assertions completely contradicted the position of the Chinese government that had been aptly prescribed in a communication sent by Peking to many Afro-Asian states in September 1963. This communication contained the following clear statement:

> the Chinese government wishes to point out that the question of revising Charter articles concerning the total number of seats in the principal United Nations organs and the question of restoring China's legitimate rights are two matters of an entirely different nature. They should not and need not be bundled together.[40]

The Afro-Asian and the Latin American states, which sponsored the above-mentioned draft resolution decided to put it to a vote. On 16 December 1963, the Special Political Committee adopted it by a roll-call of 96 to 11 with four abstentions and recommended its adoption by the General Assembly. The United States and Britain, which had previously declared that they would vote against the draft resolution, abstained along with Portugal and South Africa. The negative votes were cast by France, Cuba and the countries of the Eastern bloc. Nationalist China did not participate in the vote.

On 17 December the General Assembly in its plenary meeting discussed the draft resolution recommended by the Special Political Committee. When discussion on the draft resolution started in the General Assembly, the Soviet Union tried to bring about a postponement of a decision on the draft resolution. It recalled that none of the permanent members had voted for the draft resolution in the Special Political Committee and therefore the conditions were not propitious for the ratification of the proposed amendment by two-thirds of the UN members, including the permanent members. In its advocacy of an adjournment of the discussion, the Soviet Union laid special stress on what it considered to be China's very definite views on the substance of this matter. It warned the members of the General Assembly that 'to take action in the matter of amending the United Nations Charter without the agreement of the People's Republic of China would not only violate the Charter itself, but play into the hands of those who are concerned to create the notorious two-China situation'.[41]

The allegations that were made by the Soviet Union in the General Assembly and previously in the Special Political Committee provoked an angry reaction from Albania, which accused the Soviets of having misinformed the General Assembly about the issue. The Albanian representative in the UN stated that the Chinese government was not opposed to the expansion of Council membership. Albania characterized the Soviet allegations as 'unfounded' and called on the Soviets to 'abandon tendentious maneuvers designed to make the government of the People's Republic of

China say something that it had never said'.[42] In an attempt to show that it portrayed precisely the Chinese position, Albania drew the attention of member states to a report issued on 12 December by *Hsinhua*, a Chinese news agency that echoed the official voice of Peking. The Albanian representative in the UN quoted verbatim extracts from this report which stated that the Soviet delegate in the General Assembly completely distorted the position of communist China 'for ulterior motives'. He had also tried to sow dissension between China and the Afro-Asian states by creating the erroneous impression that the former was refusing to support the demands of the latter for Council expansion before Peking's rights in the UN were restored. The report, according to the Albanians, further stated that China is not against an expansion of the Council's membership. It also made clear that 'China's position is that it will undertake no commitment in connection with any United Nations action so long as she is apart from the United Nations'.[43]

Despite all this, the Soviet Union appealed to members of the General Assembly not to press for a vote on the draft resolution that had been approved by the Special Political Committee. The Afro-Asian states decided otherwise, however. They wanted to capitalize on two facts. First, on the fact that their draft resolution had been approved by the overwhelming majority of the member states in the Special Political Committee. Second, on the stance of Britain, France and the United States during the debate and the voting behaviour in the Special Political Committee. Neither their stance nor their voting behaviour in the Special Political Committee indicate that they opposed the reform proposal to the extent that they would block the amendment at the ratification stage. By their vote the three permanent members wanted only to express their preference for an increase in the composition of the Council by two rather than by four non-permanent seats. The ulterior motive of the Afro-Asian states was the passing of their draft resolution, if not unanimously, by the greatest possible majority. A positive vote for the draft resolution would create the political situation that was necessary for ratification of the amendments by two-thirds of the UN members, including the permanent members (Article 108 of the UN Charter).

On 17 November 1963, the draft resolution sponsored by the Afro-Asian and the Latin American states was adopted by the General Assembly as Resolution 1991A by a vote of 97 in favour and 11 against (the states of the Soviet bloc plus France) with four abstentions (Britain, United States, Portugal and South Africa). Nationalist China, which did not participate in the vote in the Special Political Committee, voted in favour of Resolution 1991A for tactical reasons, not wanting to go against the wishes of the non-aligned states who now had the numerical strength to press for its expulsion from the UN membership.[44]

By Resolution 1991A the number of non-permanent seats was increased by four non-permanent members and the total number of Security Council members was raised from 11 to 15 (five permanent and ten non-permanent members). An interesting feature of Resolution 1991 was that for the first time a clear and agreed pattern of distribution of the non-permanent seats among four different regions was promulgated. As Sam Daws, a writer on the UN, put it, 'the expansion of the Security Council . . . was a major step in the further official recognition and codification of the system of UN electoral groups'.[45] The Resolution provided that the ten non-permanent members should be elected according to the following pattern:

- five from African and Asian states;
- two from Latin American states;
- two from Western European states;
- one from Eastern European states.

The problem of ratification (1963–5)

Despite the adoption of Resolution 1991A by the General Assembly, the problem of the ratification of the Charter amendments to give effect to the expansion of the Security Council remained. First of all, there was no guarantee that the enlargement of the Council would be ratified by the five powers having the veto, as required for the enactment of UN Charter amendments. Second, the ratification of UN Charter amendments was bedevilled by political and legal problems, which needed to be solved before ratification could be legally valid. The Resolution had called on the member states to ratify the proposed amendments by September 1965. The crucial question was whether by 1965, the time limit set in the Resolution, China would in fact be in a position to ratify these amendments as a member of the UN and as a permanent member of the Security Council. Evidently, the problem of the legal ratification of the Charter amendments made the membership of the People's Republic of China in the UN a legal and political necessity within the near future. A failure to bring communist China into the UN could give a good reason to the Soviet Union to maintain its objections to Charter amendments and prevent them from entering into force.

A move that was made by the government of the People's Republic of China on 18 December 1963, the day after the passage of Resolution 1991A, paved the way for a solution that removed legal and political problems standing in the way of UN Charter amendment. In an editorial published in the 18 December issue of the Chinese newspaper *Jehmin Jih Pao*, which expressed government policy, it was stressed that 'if it proves necessary to amend the relevant articles of the United Nations Charter, we [i.e. China] shall of course, in accordance with the position which we have always taken, support such amendments so that the demand of the Afro-Asian countries can really be met'. This statement was the starting point for a complete change in the Soviet attitude. In a written statement the

Soviet Union made in the General Assembly on 21 December 1963, it referred to the statement made in *Jehmin Jih Pao* and made clear that if this statement were to be explicitly confirmed by the Government of China, Moscow 'would be prepared to agree to the amendments'. Such an official statement was never made by the Chinese government, but this did not prevent the Soviet Union from being first among the permanent members to ratify the Charter amendments in December 1964. In February 1965, it deposited its instrument of ratification with the UN urging, as Schweb wrote, 'the other great powers to do the same'. More than two-thirds of the member states, including all permanent members, deposited their instruments of ratification by the end of August 1965, the first time *de jure* Charter amendments in the history of the UN entered into force.

The Soviet government never explicitly said anything by way of explanation about the reversal of its position. It only insinuated that its previous attitude was due to the fact that it had misunderstood Peking's stand on the issue. However, this does not account for the obstructionist attitude Moscow had displayed for several years and one can only speculate as to the reasons that brought about a reversal of its position. It is clear that the Soviets' long-standing anti-reform policy had led to a severe breach between them and the rest of the UN membership. Its refusal to ratify the Charter amendments was very likely taken by the Afro-Asian states as a 'hostile' political act against them. Had this attitude continued, the long-term relationship between the Soviet and the Afro-Asian bloc would, in all probability, have become very bitter, and the margin for cooperation between them very minimal. The effect would have been to place the Soviet Union in complete isolation in the UN with severe repercussions for its policies in the world organization. With the majority of the Latin American states enjoying amicable relations with the United States,[46] the Afro-Asian states remained the only ones upon which the Soviets could possibly count for support if they were to continue to develop anti-Western policies on hot issues throughout the Cold War.

Repercussions of expansion on Council's work

A striking result of the enlarged membership of the Council was the alteration of the ratio between the number of votes required for a decision as stipulated in Article 27 of the UN Charter and the total number of members on the Council. Article 27, which originally required an affirmative vote of seven out of 11 members, was amended in 1965 to require nine votes out of 15, a serious blow to the influence of the permanent members as a group. In the earlier 11-member Council, the permanent members, if they were to act in unison, had no difficulty in easily passing a procedural or a substantive resolution by the number of votes required (i.e. seven votes). They needed to carry only two non-permanent members with them. But the 1965 amendments changed considerably the voting balance between the permanent and non-permanent members and caused serious voting complications for the former. They had to exert more effort to enlist at least four additional votes for the passing of procedural or non-procedural resolutions by nine votes, as required by the amended Article 27. Things became even worse for individual permanent members, especially after 1971, when the People's Republic took over China's seat in the UN and in the Security Council. The three Western permanent members (Britain, France and the United States) now needed the support of more than four non-permanent members to adopt a resolution, assuming the other non-Western permanent members (the Soviet Union or China) chose to refrain from exercising their veto.

In contrast, the voting power of the non-permanent members was increased so that they could now defeat any resolution. As Teja, former Deputy Permanent Representative of India to the UN, rightly observed, 'the largest gains have however accrued to the Afro-Asians who now hold an important, almost crucial voting balance'.[47] The Afro-Asian states constituted half the non-permanent membership. Alignments in the Security Council could fluctuate one way or the other depending upon the type of the issues discussed and the occupants of the non-permanent seats. However, the five Afro-Asian states had now the theoretical possibility of aligning with two fellow non-permanent members (for instance with the Latin American ones) to block a resolution, procedural or substantive. As Knight has observed 'the expansion of the Council's membership facilitated the emergence of a new coalition within that body, namely the Non-Aligned group'.[48] Indeed, the numerical strength and the political weight of NAM was remarkably increased in the expanded Council not only because of the five seats allotted to the Afro-Asian group but also because the Latin American states started from the early 1970s to join the ranks of NAM. This increased further the solidarity of the non-permanent members that did not belong to either the Western or the Eastern group and rendered NAM a significant factor in the enlarged Council.

In the enlarged Council it was difficult for any power or group to force a decision of importance. As Teja has commented, 'any positive decision by the Council requires some support from all the main blocs, East, West and the uncommitted [i.e. the non-aligned]'.[49] To overcome this problem, the Security Council, with the backing of the permanent members, began gradually from the early 1970s to move away from the confrontational formal public meetings and make use of a different method of doing business in order to arrive through negotiation and compromise at resolutions adopted by consensus or at least by an overwhelming majority: the so-called informal consultations of the whole.[50] These were private meetings of all 15 members of the Security Council that would take place away from the glare of publicity. Unlike the formal meetings, informal consultations of the whole were not preceded by the circulation of an agenda and no minutes or records of the topics discussed were kept. These meetings were secret and as such they were not open to non-members of the Council. The scheme of informal consultations gave the 15 members the chance to bypass methods of work, prescribed in the UN Charter and its own Rules of Procedure, which had rendered the Council a very cumbersome body incapable of working in its formal meetings in a business-like manner. For instance, Article 31 of the UN Charter recognized the right of any member of the UN that is not a member of the Security Council to participate without vote in the discussion of any question brought before the Security Council when the latter considers that the interests of that member are specially affected. The Security Council had hitherto applied Article 31 in a way that it became customary for it to invite 'anyone whom the majority of members wished to hear'.[51] This made the Council retreat more and more into a body that followed working practices similar to those followed by deliberative bodies such as the General Assembly. The situation was aptly described by Sir Crowe, the British Ambassador in the UN, who observed in 1977 that 'too many countries with only marginal interest in the question at issue take up the time and the physical stamina of the Council without contributing anything to the debate, often downgrading it by irrelevancies or invective'.[52]

The scheme of informal consultations was generally accepted by the members of the Council as one that paved the way for them to be engaged 'in genuine diplomacy on a broad and inter-caucus basis'.[53] It was used more frequently in the 1980s and more still in the 1990s, proving to be a very useful mechanism for diplomacy and negotiation. The official agenda of the public meetings was generally agreed in advance of such closed gatherings. In the coming years, nearly all the important resolutions that finally emerged from the public meetings of the Council were precooked and drafted in such meetings. From the account of Dedring, who served as a political officer in the UN Secretariat, what seemed to happen through the informal consultations was that

> the Council members searched in the corridors and rooms near the Council chamber for the consensus obviating the need for the veto or for voting altogether. If such a consensus position were to emerge, the Council could proceed into the formal meeting and briefly adopt what had emerged, as a result of the consultations. If no consensus was achievable, despite the lengthy and complex consultations, the matter could be abandoned before the Council needed to enter into the public phase of its diplomatic activity.[54]

1965 onward

After 1965, the membership of the UN increased significantly and by 1979 it had risen to 152, mainly due to the emergence and admission of newly independent states from Asia and the Pacific, Africa and Latin America. As a result of the further expansion of UN membership, the bloc of NAM states emerged as the most powerful group in terms of arithmetical strength. Already constituting the majority of the General Assembly, the NAM states were now proceeding with determination to exploit their arithmetical strength to press for the restructuring and democratization of the UN system. These objectives were formulated at gatherings of the NAM states in Lusaka[55] (1970), Georgetown[56] (1972), Algiers[57] (1973), Colombo[58] (1976), Havana[59] (1979) and New Delhi[60] (1983). The restructuring of the UN on the basis of the principle of democratization followed their demands: NAM members had to be placed on the decision-making mechanisms of all structures of authority that existed in the UN, not least on the Security Council. Accordingly, they viewed the issue of Security Council reform as a key step towards democratizing the UN and accommodating themselves into the decision-making process of its various organs. This prompted them to take concerted actions in order to bring about changes in the composition of the Security Council.

In 1979, India, along with 12 non-aligned states and Japan, tabled in the General Assembly a draft resolution proposing an increase in the membership of the Security Council from 15 to 19 with the addition of four non-permanent members. In that proposal the distribution of the 14 non-permanent seats was as follows: five for the African states; three for the Asian states; three for the Latin American states; two for the Western European states and others; and one for the Eastern European states. However, the permanent five and the Western and Eastern European states showed no interest in discussing the proposal. Thus, the sponsors of the draft resolution decided not to press for a vote and consideration of the item 'question of equitable representation on and increase in the membership of the Security Council' was postponed to the 1980 session[61] and, following that, deferred in all the subsequent sessions of the General Assembly (from 1980 to 1990).[62] The early 1980s were marked by growing hostility between the United States and the Soviet Union and, as a result, the permanent five and other states were unwilling to discuss the substance of the item. The issue of Council reform resurfaced with great vigour in the early 1990s as the astonishing scope of changes in the world opened up an improved prospect of commitment by the member states to reform of the Security Council.

3 The post-Cold War case for reform

The new international setting and the impulse for reform

Demands for reform of the Security Council have been growing for years. In fact, the issue of Council reform had been on the General Assembly's agenda since 1979 but had attracted little interest. However, Security Council reform became a 'hot issue' in the late 1980s when the end of East–West confrontation opened up prospects for a greater role of the Security Council in world affairs.

Indeed, from the mid-1980s, major developments occurred in world politics that changed significantly the international political environment within which the UN had been operating for years. Beginning with the coming to power of Gorbachev in 1985, events such as the fall of the Berlin Wall in 1989, German unification, the collapse of communist rule in Central and Eastern Europe, and the dissolution of the Warsaw Pact, led the two opposing blocs, East and West, to come closer together and leave aside old hatreds and ideological intransigence. Such epoch-making events put the UN in a totally different position from that it had previously occupied. The climate of cooperation resulting from the rapprochement of long-time adversaries was closer to the ideal held by the founders of the UN than at any time since the end of the Second World War. This situation gave rise to the hope, expressed by various members of the world organization, that the potential of the Security Council, which had been held hostage by the Cold War, would now be released and the UN would be better able to function as it was intended to.

Following these trends, a radical change in Soviet attitudes towards the UN further paved the way for the rejuvenation of the Security Council. While the Cold War period was characterized by cynical indifference on behalf of the Soviet Union towards the UN and the purposes for which it was intended, the revolutionary nature of Gorbachev's leadership had a direct impact on Soviet perception of the UN. In 1987 The Soviet leader gave the UN pride of place in his 'new thinking' about Soviet foreign policy. In fact, one of the key themes of Gorbachev's 'new thinking' on international relations was a greatly expanded and enhanced role for the

UN in international politics.[1] The UN became an important part of post-Cold War Soviet policy to which Gorbachev in particular was much committed.[2] During his leadership the Soviet Union advanced a greater number of proposals for strengthening the UN and in particular the Security Council than any other member state. He called for a central role for the UN, with special emphasis on the Security Council, in providing a comprehensive system of global security.[3] In the words of Shevardnadze, the Soviet Foreign Minister, 'the most important thing [for Soviet foreign policy] is to preserve the type of order in which all decisions related to upholding international society are made by the UN Security Council, in which we have a veto right'.[4] Elements of this new Soviet policy toward the UN included the enlargement of the role of UN peacekeeping forces and the revival of the moribund Military Staff Committee, composed of the chiefs of staff of the five permanent members.[5] In his speech to the UN General Assembly on 7 December 1998, Gorbachev reasserted 'the supremacy of the common human idea over the countless multiplicity of centrifugal forces', and expressed regret that the UN had become 'for many years a field for cultivating political confrontation'.[6]

Iraq's invasion of Kuwait was an opportunity to test this new era of collective security. Russia's full backing of the UN Security Council resolutions for economic sanctions and the use of force against Iraq in 1990 and 1991 was the most tangible indication of the new commitment to international cooperation. After years of using its veto in the Security Council as an instrument of counter-policy towards the West, the Soviets had committed to transforming the UN from 'an arena for the Cold War' to 'a field for really constructive cooperation'.[7]

The attitude of the Soviet Union towards the UN and the Security Council in particular was inextricably linked with its search for a new role after the loss of its empire and status as a global superpower. Its collapsing economy, the huge loss of population and territories, its military shortcomings and serious domestic problems constrained its international role and had a dramatic impact on the course of its new foreign policy. Its foreign policy was thereafter informed by the desire to compensate for the loss of its superpower status and to counter its marginal role within the international system.[8] Not surprisingly, its attitude towards the UN evolved accordingly. The UN, and the Security Council in particular, was now perceived as the sole arena in which it could wield power on the international scene.

Having accorded the UN, and especially the Security Council, a primary role in its foreign policy, the Soviet Union under Gorbachev chose to work closely with the United States and the other permanent members in the Security Council and to avoid splits within it where possible. No longer possessing the voice of a superpower, the Soviet Union had begun virtually seconding the West's stand on almost everything. Cooperation with the West – particularly through the UN – was seen as a means of affirming the

Soviet Union's great power status. Gorbachev, and his successor Yeltsin, believed that by following a pro-Western policy, their country would win international recognition.[9] Characteristically, in his address to the UN in early 1992, President Yeltsin stated that Russia regarded the Western countries as 'allies'.[10] The desire for consensus with the West was evident in the dramatic decline in Russian vetoes in the Security Council.[11] The Chinese, too, 'were well disposed towards cooperation with the four other permanent members'.[12] As Taylor wrote, the Chinese 'were anxious to re-establish their reputation after the disaster of Tienanmen Square, and were also keen to demonstrate that they were worthy of Western economic aid'.[13]

These changes in the attitudes of the Soviet Union and China brought about an air of unity and rediscovered cooperation among the UN members, especially the five permanent members of the Security Council. As a result, they found themselves able to agree to engage in a large number of regional conflicts, such as the Iran–Iraq war and the crises over Nicaragua, El Salvador, Cambodia and Namibia. Perhaps the Gulf War provided the most conclusive evidence of cooperation among the permanent five. For the first time since the Korean War (1950–3), the Security Council was able to invoke Chapter VII to undertake military action against a state it deemed to be an aggressor. Due to the relatively high degree of accord among the five permanent members, the Security Council suddenly became extremely effective and started working at full steam. From the early 1990s, it began to launch an unprecedented number and range of peace operations, to meet more frequently than in the past and to pass more resolutions than ever before in its history,[14] thus emerging as a powerful actor in areas of conflict or potential conflict.

As the Security Council began to play a more active role in dealing with situations relating to international peace and security and world attention was preoccupied more than ever with the work of the Council, the case for restructuring the most important organ of the UN gained momentum. Critics of the status quo argued that the composition, distribution of permanent and non-permanent seats and distribution of power and influence in the Security Council reflected the reality of the world of 1945. Hence there have been persistent complaints that the Council's decisions did not reflect the will of the international community as a whole but rather the will of the few who dominate it because of their disproportionate representation in the Council's membership.

These events, along with the emergence of Japan, Germany and the European Union as global economic powers, the relative decline of Great Britain and France from global to middle-ranking powers and the large increase in UN membership, fuelled the simmering debate on the reform of the Security Council.

Thus, from the onset of the 1990s, a reunited Germany and a reformed Japan started clamouring for permanent membership on the Council, reasonably claiming, although unofficially, as much right as Britain and

France to sit as permanent members. The fear that elevating Germany to permanent member status would be tantamount to Italy's decline to a power of second rank[15] prompted Rome to raise the issue of the European Community's representation on the Security Council. The idea was floated that a seat could be introduced for the then European Community, which should be allowed to speak with only one voice in the Security Council. This idea owes its origin to Gianni de Michelis, the Italian Foreign Minister, who, in September 1990, suggested that Britain and France should step down in favour of one permanent seat for the European Community and one permanent seat for Japan. As an ardent supporter of European political unification, Italy believed that its proposal, if adopted, could lead to a stronger Common Foreign and Security Policy of the Community.[16] De Michelis also suggested that the issue of European collective representation in the UN should be addressed in the context of the Intergovernmental Conference on Political Union (April 1991), which should focus, *inter alia*, on the realization of a common seat for the Twelve on the Security Council.[17]

Furthermore, a large number of states – mostly from the less developed world – started forwarding their demands for a reform of the Council that would better reflect the geographical distribution of UN membership. They declared their deep dissatisfaction with the Council's unrepresentative character and arrogant exercise of power by the permanent five. The admission of a large number of states from Central and Eastern Europe as well as Yugoslavia to the UN family increased criticism, not least from the group of the non-aligned states, that the present Council no longer retained its representative character, as it represented only a fraction of the UN membership. The Security Council, it was often argued, was not numerically proportionate to the General Assembly membership as a whole and it would lose the trust and faith of the overall membership unless it achieved a more balanced representation. It is noteworthy that by 1946 the UN had 51 members, 11 of whom were members of the Security Council. The increase in the membership of the Council to 15 in 1963 was a response to the increasing membership in the UN, which, from 113 in that year (the year of the last increase in the Council's membership), rose to 183 in the beginning of the 1990s. Complaints were also directed against the five permanent members of the Council. As Morphet notes, 'points made [by several non-aligned states] in 1990 were a concern over the dictatorship of the permanent members'.[18]

The five permanent members of the Security Council reacted very guardedly to the prospects of reforming the body. The most obvious reason was their reluctance to share their privileged position with others and/or fear of losing their position, which they saw as a symbol of their international status and prestige. They reached a tacit agreement and adopted a common stance on the reform issue: to resist claims for reform and to do their utmost to prevent discussion on the subject in the UN.

The successful involvement of the Council in the Gulf crisis (August 1990 to January 1991) gave the permanent five the chance, on the one hand, to further cement their bonds of commonality and, on the other hand, to use the 'efficiency' argument behind which they rallied in order to justify their objection to Council reform. Understandably, the United States and Britain pointed to the Security Council's action over the Gulf War as proof that the existing Council was now working well and there was no need to amend its membership. The Soviets and the French, in an attempt to add their own voice of opposition to the demands for Council reform, started to back the 'efficiency' argument, which was expressed in the American slogan, 'if it ain't broke, don't fix it', or its British version, 'why change a winning team'. As the Soviets put it, 'the organization cannot afford to engage in an overhaul of machinery which not only is not broken but is in fact in good working order'.[19] The French also seized the opportunity to declare shortly after the Gulf War that 'there was not sufficient grounds for a retroactive reading of the UN Charter to take into account developments since 1945'.[20]

The permanent five, either collectively or singularly, brought their influence to bear upon the members of the world organization with a view to averting debate on Council reform in the UN during the period from 1990 to mid-1992. Thus, they managed to defeat a UN resolution requesting discussion of the issue in the General Assembly in September 1991. The resolution had been tabled by India, Brazil and eight other countries, following a meeting of the NAM at Accra where the foreign ministers of the movement for reform called for a review of the membership on the Council.[21] The issue was deferred to the next session of the UN General Assembly that was to take place in September 1992.[22]

The reluctance of Germany and Japan openly to pursue permanent seats for themselves during the period 1990–1 facilitated the permanent five's task of containing debate on the Council reform issue. The question of their representation on the Security Council had been one of the 'unspoken and burning issues' in the foreign and security policy of Germany and Japan.[23] Both had begun since 1990 viewing the Security Council as a vehicle for a more active role in world affairs but, for various and almost similar reasons, they appeared reluctant to claim a permanent seat officially.

First, as the Gulf crisis mounted at the end of 1990, Bonn and Tokyo did not want to press hard on an issue that might have jeopardized their relations with France, Britain and the United States at a time when they, with the UN's blessings, had taken full-scale economic and military action against Iraq. Second, as scholars have pointed out the political debate within Germany and Japan over their role in international security 'somewhat dampened' their respective government's resolve to press the issue. Indeed, policy-makers and a significant segment of the German and the Japanese public had serious reservations about the prospect of their respective countries assuming a greater share of responsibility in the UN. Third, Germany and Japan were taking a 'wait and see' posture in order to ascertain the reaction of the permanent members of the Security Council – especially Britain and France – towards the demands of the developing states for Council reform. Germany also held off, waiting for Japan to go public with its candidature for permanent membership. As Drift put it, 'the German government had gained the impression that the Japanese side was well on the way to achieving a consensus on the issue and seemed to be on the verge of going public about it'.[24] The anticipated bids for permanent seats by Germany and Japan were partly complementary because of the similarity in the economic and political importance of the two countries and this caused Germany to wait for the reaction of the international community, and especially of the permanent five, to the Japanese candidature. Similarly, Japan waited to see how the permanent five and Germany would react to the Italian proposal to replace Britain and France with Japan and the EU. The Italian proposal (permanent five minus two plus two), although beset with legal and political problems, had the advantage of keeping the Council the same size. As such, it would also have the advantage of being unlikely seriously to diminish the Council's effectiveness. Japan believed that Italy's proposal would be politically more acceptable to a majority of UN members and especially to the non-aligned states. As one scholar put it, 'it is difficult to see how they [the non-aligned states] could oppose a reform that reduced the total West European representation even if it did not increase their own, and which ensured the inclusion in the permanent membership of one of the UN's most important members, at least in financial terms'.[25]

However, Britain and France, who fervently defended their permanent five status as a symbol of their role in world affairs, not only did not express support for the Italian proposal but they avoided discussing it with their European partners at the EU fora.[26] Both prevented the Intergovernmental Conference (April 1990 to April 1991), which led to the signing of the Treaty on European Union in Maastricht, from addressing the issue and both wanted to insert a provision in the Maastricht Treaty providing that

> member states [of the EU] which are also members of the Security Council will act in concert and keep other member states fully informed. Member states which are permanent members of the Security Council will, in the execution of their functions, ensure the defence of their positions and the interests of the European Union, without prejudice of their responsibilities under the provisions of the UN Charter.[27]

Thus, Britain and France managed to have their special status on the Security Council recognized by their European partners. The insertion of the J5.4 provision in the Maastricht Treaty indicated the willingness of the two states to dissuade their European partners from discussing the issue of EU representation on the Security Council in the future. As Minister Garel Jones, on behalf of the British government, stated in the European Parliament in 1992, there was no need to change the existing arrangements in the Security Council because they offered a satisfactory representation for Europe. 'Europe has two permanent members on the Security Council and that gives Europe a powerful voice in the international arena', he said. This voice, he added, is further strengthened by the election of an EU member to the non-permanent seat allocated to Western Europe. 'Europe has a strong voice on the Security Council and we want to be very careful before we seek to tamper with that',[28] he added.

It is worth mentioning at this point that a collective EU seat on the Security Council, apart from the obvious boost it would have given to the process of European integration, would have also provided Germany, as a member of the EU, with a voice within the Security Council and, most importantly, would have fulfilled its wishes for an equal footing (*Gleichberechtigung*) with Britain and France on the Council. But Germany avoided taking a position on the Italian proposal and decided against raising the issue during the EU's Intergovernmental Conference. The real reason was simple: the Italian proposal would not have addressed German aspirations. Germany wanted more international responsibility as a permanent member, and representation on the Security Council in common with its European partners would not have provided that responsibility.

A *de facto* reform of the Security Council: Russia slips into the Soviet seat

While the permanent members continued to act in concert to contain the debate on Council reform in the UN, the collapse of the Soviet Union in December 1991 brought with it uncertainty about its permanent seat on the Council. In late December 1991, the USSR was formally dissolved through the mutual recognition of the independence of its constituent republics and the creation by most of them of the CIS.

The dissolution of the Soviet Union raised the important question of what was to happen to the Soviet seat on the Security Council. Would Russia be a state successor to the USSR with respect to its membership in the UN and its permanent seat in the Security Council? With the demise of the 'Union of Soviet Socialist Republics' this name had to be expunged from Article 23 of the UN Charter.

It has to be acknowledged that there was no precedent for handling such a contingency in the UN context. Only once before, in 1971, had a Security Council permanent seat changed hands. At that time the issue of the Chinese seat on the Security Council was resolved by being treated as a matter of credentials, that is, of representation rather than of membership. There was one recognized state, China, which was indisputably entitled to UN membership and to a Security Council permanent seat. Subsequently, the only question was which government was legally entitled to speak for that country, the old nationalist one, now only in control of Taiwan, or Mao's well-entrenched communist government. Following the failure of the United States to at least secure a General Assembly seat (that is regular UN membership) for the Taiwan regime, the latter was evicted from the world body and the People's Republic of China was confirmed as the sole representative of 'China'.[29] Perhaps the Soviet Union/Russia case bears a closer resemblance to that of a state splitting apart, where a former 'composite state' breaks up into several parts. Two examples are the separation of India and Pakistan in 1947 and Pakistan and Bangladesh in 1971, where the larger unit, which also continued to bear the former corporate name, kept the General Assembly seat and continued UN membership. The resulting new entity, by contrast, had to reapply for membership, going through the standard procedure stipulated in Article 4 of the UN Charter. In none of these cases, though, was a UN Security Council permanent seat involved.

From a legal point of view, the Alma Ata agreement, which gave birth to the CIS, complicated the replacement of the USSR with the Russian Federation. The agreement explicitly stated that 'with the establishment of the Commonwealth of Independent States, the Union of Soviet Socialists Republics cease[d] to exist'.[30] A more legally correct approach, which would have left no room for any challenge to the Russian claim on USSR succession, would have been for all Soviet republics but Russia to have formally declared their secession from the Union. Such a move would have identified Russia, at least for a while, with the Union, and would have thus made this case fall neatly under the India–Pakistan precedent. Once recognized as the natural heir to all the Union's rights and obligations, the 'Russian Soviet Union' could have easily proceeded to change its name without a Charter amendment. Such a subtle choreography may have been unthinkable under the rushed circumstances and the symbolic and domestic political needs of the ruling elites of the various former Soviet republics. For the sake of appearances, however, it became clear soon after Alma Ata that the Soviet Union could not just vanish – there was a need for continuity. Thus we get the careful wording from the European Community which, in its statement of 23 December 1991, refrained from using the term 'recognition' with regard to Russia, unlike its position with regard to the other former Soviet republics. The reason for this special treatment was that the state members of the European Community 'accepted Russia's continuity of the international personality of the Soviet Union'.[31]

The Russians were concerned about the implications of Russia not being automatically considered as the rightful successor to the Soviet

Union and being obliged to go through the usual procedure of applying as an aspiring member. If the admission stipulations of Article 4 of the UN Charter were to be followed, the Russian issue had ultimately to be discussed and decided upon within the framework of the General Assembly.[32]

President Yeltsin took swift action to ensure a smooth transition from a Soviet to a Russian permanent seat on the Council. He put pressure on the CIS heads of states to 'support Russia's continuance of the membership of the USSR in the UN, including permanent membership of the Security Council, and other international organizations'.[33] On 20 December, 1991, he sent a letter to President Bush stating that 'the end of the existence of the USSR as a subject of international law require[s] that ... the question of the Security Council permanent member'[s] seat be urgently addressed'.[34] Subsequently, in a letter dated 24 December 1991, he informed the UN Secretary-General that 'the membership of the Union of Socialist republics in the UN, including the Security Council and the other organs and organizations of the UN system, is being continued by the Russian Federation with the support of the countries of the Commonwealth of Independent States'. The letter was immediately circulated among the UN membership and received *de facto* acceptance, as no objection was raised.[35] Thus, the UN was presented with a *fait accompli*. The move conveniently took place once the General Assembly had completed the substantive discussions of its 46th session and left no room for examination of or questioning the issue. Informally, though, it was received with mixed feelings and even bitterness by the diplomatic community.[36] In any case, a physical semblance of continuity was also projected by Yeltsin's decision to appoint Vorontsov, who had been permanent representative of the USSR, as permanent representative of Russia to the UN. All in all, the result was that 'Russia ... has without debate or a vote 'inherited' the USSR seat in the Security Council'.[37] The formula used precluded any substantive discussion of the real issues involved.[38]

The explicit acceptance by the majority of the former Soviet republics and major international actors of Russia's continuity of the international personality of the Soviet Union constituted the strongest legal argument in favour of the USSR's succession by Russia, at least in the UN context. John Major, Prime Minister of Britain, rushed to send a letter to Yeltsin on 23 December stating that Her Majesty's Government recognized 'the continuity of statehood between Russia and the former USSR'.[39] The European Community and its member states at the same time 'noted that the international rights and obligations of the former USSR, including those under the UN Charter, would continue to be exercised by Russia'.[40] President Bush, in his victorious 'Address to the Nation on the Commonwealth of Independent States' on Christmas Day (25 December) 1991, announcing the end of the Soviet Union, had this to say: '[W]e will support Russia's assumption of the USSR's seat as a permanent member of the UN Security Council'.[41]

The dual agenda of the 1992 Security Council summit

The only thing missing at this point was a symbolic high-profile move that would seal the transition from the USSR to Russia and would confer upon the latter a final *de facto* recognition of its right to succeed the former Soviet Union, especially as a Security Council permanent member. As the best way to go about it, it was suggested that a Security Council summit be held in January 1992.[42] It was Britain, a trusted member of the permanent five and a most interested one, which took the initiative in realizing a Security Council summit, an idea originally floated in 1991 by France, the other equally concerned permanent member. The timing was propitious, as the British were due to hold the Council's rotating presidency in January 1992, immediately after the December dissolution of the Soviet Union. Thus, the Council held, for the first time in its history, a summit on 31 January 1992, seemingly to consider the role of the Council in the post-Cold War era, but, in reality, to confirm Russia resolutely as the rightful successor of the Soviet Union.[43] Thirteen heads of state or government (Britain, France, China, the Russian Federation, the United States, Austria, Belgium, Cape Verde, Ecuador, India, Japan, Morocco and Venezuela) and two foreign ministers (Hungary and Zimbabwe) met at the headquarters of the UN in New York.

Russia's claim to the Security Council permanent seat was a delicate issue for the Council's permanent membership, especially for Britain and France. A discussion of the Russian issue in the General Assembly might have prompted a debate by the whole UN membership and called into question the composition of the Security Council. It might also have led to a confrontation on Council reform, at a time when a large number of states were calling for changes in its structure. Moreover, it could have raised the question of the legitimacy of states like Britain and France – who, in the post-Second World War period, had declined from global to middle-ranking powers – having permanent seats on the Council (with the associated veto prerogative). This explains why 'the British needed the question of the permanent five sewn up quickly' (as did the French for that matter).[44]

The legal-diplomatic 'coup', by which the Soviet seat was passed to Russia, was executed with the active involvement of the other permanent members (which had good reason to want to defer any re-examination of the Council's composition and powers indefinitely) and with the apparent acquiescence of the Council's non-permanent members. The Americans seemed to concur, also favouring '[a] quick and uncontested transfer of representation',[45] while the Chinese 'remained somewhat aloof ... but stopped short of being obstructive'.[46] It is worth recalling that the Security Council's Provisional Rules of Procedure allow the President to call such a meeting of the Council at any time he or she deems necessary or at the request of any member. However, although the

President (Britain, in this case) can exercise his or her influence, he or she cannot insist upon a meeting to discuss a particular matter in the absence of a consensus among the permanent five. As Scharf, a State Department lawyer, put it

> [t]he other members of the permanent five worried that any change to the Soviet seat would set off a scramble by other countries for Security Council reform ... [They] thus had an interest in ensuring that changes to Soviet membership in the United Nations would not produce challenges to other features of the Security Council, such as the permanent five/rotating ten number and composition, the inseparability of the veto from a permanent seat, and the non-rotation of permanent members ... In particular [they] ... feared that leaving the Soviet seat vacant would be seen as an open invitation to other members to push their proposals for expanding or altering the composition of the permanent five.[47]

President Yeltsin was invited to and participated in the meeting as the head of a state that *de facto* enjoyed permanent membership status. It is worth noting that in addressing the Council, President Yeltsin, fully aware of the real purpose of the summit, emphasized that 'Russia is prepared to continue partnership between the permanent members of the Security Council'.[48] Furthermore, he pointed out that the Russian Federation is 'a state with centuries-long experience in foreign policy and diplomacy'.[49] He concluded by expressing his confidence that 'the world community will find in Russia, as an equal participant in international relations and as a permanent member of the Security Council, a firm and steadfast champion of freedom, democracy and humanism.'[50] In response to Yeltsin's remarks, the President of the Council, British Prime Minister Major, took the floor immediately following the Russian President's speech in order to state pointedly: 'Mr. President ... I know the Council would wish me to welcome Russia as a permanent member of our Council. You are welcome indeed'.[51] That was it: the gavel hit the table and the time for any objections from whatever quarter had passed. The predominant objective of the summit – to ensure a smooth transition from a Soviet to a Russian permanent seat on the Security Council – had been won. The summit had managed to legitimize, in the eyes of the international community, Russia as the successor to the USSR as permanent member.

It is not surprising that all five permanent members kept silent on the thorny issue of Security Council reform during the summit session. In contrast, several non-permanent members, including Japan and India, did refer to the subject, if only briefly. The Japanese Prime Minister Miyazawa conceded that the Soviet Union's seat should be taken by the Russian Federation, but seized the opportunity to distance himself from the permanent five stating that it is necessary for the United Nations to evolve while adapting to a changing world. For example, certain sections of the United Nations Charter are based on the realities prevailing in 1945, when the United Nations was founded, which predate even the Cold War. In addition, since the Security Council is at the centre of United Nations efforts to maintain international peace and security, it is important to consider thoroughly ways to adjust its functions, composition and other aspects so as to make it more reflective of the realities of the new era. This is a process in which Japan is prepared to take an active part.[52]

In a way, Japan's demands for a permanent seat were pre-empted by the Security Council summit that occurred at an inopportune moment for that country. Japan was still undergoing internal adjustments to ease constitutional constraints on its participation in military operations abroad (the famous Article 9 of the Japanese constitution).

As far as Germany was concerned, it did not raise objections to the way the Russian issue was handled through the Security Council summit. British diplomats were fully justified in their anticipation that there would be no reaction on Germany's part with regard to the USSR–Russia succession. As a British official put it in the early days of January 1992: '[S]ince the Germans have been calling more than anyone else for the need to involve Russia on the international stage, they could hardly fail to be satisfied by a proposal to bring President Yeltsin to New York and Russia on to the Council as quickly as possible'.[53] Moreover, much like Japan, Germany at that time was not in a position to 'fight' for a Security Council permanent seat, due to its own constitutional ambiguities regarding military missions abroad.[54] It should be noted that Moscow was the only permanent member that had raised the issue of a German permanent seat at the Security Council as early as September 1990.

As previously stated, the summit of 31 January 1992 had a dual agenda, with a hidden as well as a public part. It has been argued that the main item on the hidden agenda was the confirmation, beyond any doubt or potential challenge, of Russia as the rightful successor to the USSR's permanent seat on the Security Council. The official agenda of the summit consisted of one sole item, namely, *The Responsibility of the Security Council in the Maintenance of International Peace and Security*. John Major, the president of the Council, made it more specific by presenting the 'the four important purposes' that this extraordinary meeting which his country had convened was supposed to serve:

1   to mark the beginning of a new era for the world and for the UN;
2   to reaffirm the commitment of the Council members to the UN Charter principles, especially collective security, through which all threats to international peace and security should be dealt with;

3   to update and develop the means – such as preventive action, peace-making and peacekeeping – by which collective security is upheld through the United Nations, and to provide the necessary resources to the United Nations and its Secretary-General, with a view to enhancing their ability to handle crises; and

4   to renew the international commitment to arms control.[55]

The speeches of the 15 world leaders revolved around the above topics, plus other issues of global importance, such as economic development, human rights and protection of the environment. In fact, what each leader did was to offer a kind of wish list, a brief account of what should be done by the world body considering these new, more propitious circumstances. Overall, proposals on how to achieve the suggested goals did not go far beyond broad references to UN revitalization and use of the full UN Charter potential, now presumably within reach. The printed proceedings of the meeting read more like the ceremonial General Assembly annual introductory session known as 'general debate' rather than of a business-like meeting of world leaders who were expected to come up with innovative ideas on how best to organize the Security Council with a view to responding effectively to, among other challenges, post-Cold War disputes, conflicts and crises.

The summit ended with the adoption of a declaration unanimously approved by the Security Council members and read out as a presidential statement by the British Prime Minister. The declaration referred to the opportunities but also to the risks brought by this new 'time of change'; reviewed some of the positive steps already taken (e.g. the operation against Iraq and the addition of elements, such as election monitoring and human rights verification, to the tasks already performed by UN peace-keeping forces); and underlined the need for all UN members to fulfil their obligations with regard to arms control and disarmament. The members of the Security Council pledged their commitment to international law and to the UN Charter, especially with regard to the peaceful settlement of disputes and collective security. In other words, the members of the Security Council did not produce much more than a loosely phrased declaration of good intentions. In the most operative part of the declaration, the Council membership

> invite[d] the Secretary-General to prepare, for circulation to the members of the UN by July 1992, his analysis and recommendations on ways of strengthening and making more efficient within the framework and provisions of the Charter the capacity of the UN for preventive diplomacy, for peacemaking and for peacekeeping.

By delegating to the Secretary-General the responsibility to make a comprehensive analysis and recommendations, the members of the Council avoided entering into specific commitments themselves vis-à-vis the official agenda item. The much-acclaimed report, *An Agenda for Peace*,[56] produced by Boutros Ghali in June 1992, together with its 1995 sequel, *Supplement to an Agenda for Peace*,[57] had more of an impact on the intellectual and conceptual sphere than on the practical one. This transfer of responsibility by the Council members to the Secretary-General provides further evidence in support of the argument that the heads of state or government of the five permanent members of the Council had not come to the summit with the objective of having a substantive discussion about ways and means of strengthening the role of the Security Council in the post-Cold War era. Apparently this was not the intention of the convenor of the summit, namely, Britain, and its closest collaborators, the United States and France. As previously stated, their main objective was to ensure the quick transition from a Soviet to a Russian seat on the Council.

However, the summit did achieve one objective of the permanent members who had agreed to participate: to demonstrate to the UN members and the public at large that the post-Cold War Council was working in harmony and, consequently, that no changes to its structure, composition and functioning were warranted. This viewpoint deftly found its way into the text of the joint declaration adopted at the end of the 31 January summit: The members of the Security Council consider that there are new favourable international circumstances under which the Security Council has begun to fulfil more effectively its primary responsibility for the maintenance of international peace and security.[58]

4   The debate in the UN: 1992–5

By allowing Russia to take over the permanent seat of the former Soviet Union in the Security Council, the permanent members hoped that the reform issue 'was shelved for another decade'.[1] However, their hopes were short-lived. Germany and Japan changed their policy and began publicly to voice their aspirations to become permanent members, while the non-aligned states increased their determination to implement Council reform.

Following the success of the Gulf War, Germany and Japan were hopeful that the UN, especially the Security Council, would play an important role in maintaining international peace and security in the post-Cold War era. As a result, public opposition in both these countries to calls for a permanent seat was significantly reduced, which led to the opening of a public debate on the removal of constitutional impediments prohibiting the use of troops in overseas operations. Coupled with the significant financial support given by both countries to the Gulf War, Germany and Japan strengthened their case for permanent membership and, by 1992, became more insistent on it.

The strength of Germany's and Japan's desire to become permanent members of the Security Council can be seen in their willingness to bear a greater share of the UN's financial burden, which had grown dramatically since the 1980s. By 1992, Japan and Germany had become, respectively, the second and third largest contributors to the regular budget of the UN, and to the costs for peacekeeping operations as well. Japan paid an average of 12.5 per cent of the total cost while Germany contributed about 8.93 per cent to the UN's budget and to the expenses for the peacekeeping operations. This was almost the average contribution of the permanent five. According to UN reports in 1992, the five permanent members of the Security Council paid 46.50 per cent of the regular budget of the UN, with the United States paying the lion's share of 25 per cent.[2] Russia, France and Britain paid 9.41, 6.0 and 5.2 per cent, respectively, while China paid only 0.77 per cent. The permanent five also paid 55.80 per cent of the costs of all UN peacekeeping operations. The growing financial burden which Japan and Germany shouldered in 1992 led them to believe that, since they were major contributors in paying the UN piper, they should also call some of the tunes. As Yoshio Hatano, the Japanese Ambassador to the UN pointed out, 'in the future we do not want to be just good tax-payers, but to have a word to say on the important decisions that are taken in the United Nations'.[3]

Council reform was also one of the main issues discussed by the members of the NAM in Jakarta at their summit in September 1992. These states expressed concern 'over the tendency of some states to dominate the Council' as well as the view that 'the veto powers which guarantee an exclusive and dominant role for the permanent members of the Council are contrary to the aim of democratizing the United Nations and must, therefore, be reviewed'. They were determined to play a leading role in the revitalization of the UN and pressed hard to get the Council's membership to reflect the increased membership of the UN as a whole.[4]

India, and 35 other non-aligned states, undertook to implement the decision reached at Jakarta. They tabled, in September 1992, a draft resolution that called for the inclusion in the provisional agenda of the 48th session of the General Assembly, an item entitled 'Question of equitable representation on and increase in the membership of the Security Council'. The permanent five could no longer contain discussion of the issue. On 11 December, the draft resolution, which was co-sponsored by Japan, was adopted without vote as Resolution 47/62. The resolution placed the question of Council reform on the agenda of the General Assembly, where it has since remained. It also requested member states to submit by the summer of 1993 written comments 'on a possible review of the membership of the Security Council'.[5] In 1993, 80 states sent written comments[6] and another 74 made their views known verbally during the 48th session of the General Assembly.[7] The positions adopted indicated clearly the urgency for the Security Council reform. Later that year, the General Assembly, in Resolution 48/26, set up the Open-Ended Working Group to consider all aspects of the question of Council reform.[8] Thus began the debate on the reform of the Security Council that continues to the present day.

Conditional support for Germany and Japan

At the beginning of the debate, the club's weakest permanent members, Britain and France, were quick to reject Council reform. They argued that maintaining the Council's operational efficiency was a higher priority than enlarging its membership. A protracted debate on enlargement, the British warned, could impair the Council's effectiveness. 'The first priority', according to the British, 'must be to safeguard the effective operation of the Council and its ability to fulfil its primary responsibility under the UN Charter'.[9] France used similar arguments to defend the status quo. The Council's effectiveness, said the French, stems from its limited membership, which permits it to achieve compromise, reach decisions more easily and respond rapidly to crises throughout the world. France saw no reason for enlarging the Council since 'the 10 non-permanent members of the Council already ensure an equitable geographical representation of member states, and they have contributed to the Council's primary role now at last restored to its original character'.[10] For its part Russia kept a low profile on the issue but its position was basically the same as that of Britain and France. It emphasized improving the Council's working methods rather than expanding its membership.[11] China took an ambiguous position since on the one hand, it recognized that there was a need for membership expansion while, on the other hand, admitting that the time was not ripe.[12]

Surprisingly, the only permanent member that expressed support for expansion was the United States. In the summer of 1993, the United States differentiated its position from that of the other four permanent members. It abandoned its previous opposition to the Council reform and called for Germany and Japan to become permanent members. In June 1993 the United States stated that

> the current permanent members of the Council are countries with global and economic influence and a capacity as well as a will to contribute to global peace and security through peacekeeping and other activities. Their status on the Council should remain unaltered. The United States supports permanent membership for Japan and Germany as well, fully recognizing that permanent membership entails assuming an active role in global peace and security activities.[13]

American support for Germany and Japan did not amount to unconditional endorsement. The United States made it clear that, in return for permanent membership, Germany and Japan would have to pull their own financial weight as well as be willing to participate in peacekeeping operations and discharge other global responsibilities.

This policy reversal put pressure on Britain and France to change their position. Both now feared that continued opposition to Council reform would do more harm than good since they would remain the only Western states objecting to expansion. After receiving assurances from the United States that there would be no change in the status of the existing permanent members, they began to soften their position. Thus, Britain, in the summer of 1993, and France, in the spring of 1994, gave lukewarm support to Germany's and Japan's candidacy as the lesser of two evils, the alternative being a collective EU seat, a proposal that had been presented in the discussions about Council reform as the only one of all propositions that would result in the removal of Britain and France from the Council. With British and French support for Bonn, the prospects of a collective EU seat on the Security Council became more remote. Smaller European states, who would have been the chief beneficiaries had the EU obtained a seat on the Council, withdrew their support for the Italian proposal and turned to other reform proposals, not least of which was support for Germany's candidacy.[14] Thus, the issue of EU representation in the Security Council was put on the back burner. During the EU's Intergovernmental Conference in Amsterdam in 1996–7, several members of the European Parliament made a futile effort to re-posit the issue, but Carlos Westendrop, the President-in-Office of the European Council at that time, stated that the Intergovernmental Conference 'would not be the appropriate venue' in which to discuss the issue. He argued that the EU 'does not have a common position on this matter'.[15] Indeed, the Intergovernmental Conference proved to be a highly 'inappropriate venue' for deliberation since its constitutional underpinning, the Amsterdam Treaty on European Union, stipulated that it was required to follow the provisions of the Maastricht Treaty in dealing with EU representation on the Security Council.

However, the most important reason for the Anglo-French change in position was probably the fact that the United States had not yet backed Germany's and Japan's candidacy without reservation. Britain and France aligned themselves with the American position. They expressed satisfaction with the increased financial support of the two countries to the UN, but they also made it clear that their participation in UN military operations must be considered as well in evaluating their candidacies. This was reiterated on several occasions by the British and French diplomats and officials in various UN organs and in other international forums. In 1993, Douglas Hurd, the British Foreign Secretary, said that agreement to the accession of Germany and Japan to permanent membership could be reached only when the two countries were fully involved in peacekeeping operations.[16] In April 1994, his French counterpart, Alain Juppe, similarly stated that 'all those who aspire to be permanent members of the Security Council must accept all the obligations as well as the rights. I am thinking here about peacekeeping operations'.[17]

These official public statements, carefully crafted for the record, meant that Britain and France were following a 'wait-and-see' policy based on the two countries' taking the necessary steps to meet the so-called military criterion for permanent membership that had been laid down by them and the United States. They also meant that permanent membership was still far from certain because it was dependent on the ability of the two candidates to shoulder the military responsibilities that such membership entailed. The Russian and Chinese position had changed little. Beginning in 1994, they went on record as supporting Council reform but continued to maintain a low profile on the issue and avoided openly supporting the candidacy of any country.[18]

Japan and Germany were not satisfied with the position of Britain, France and the United States, not only because of the conditional acceptance of their candidacies, but also because of their silence on the question of the right of veto. Their non-committal position on the veto issue led Germany to state that it would not accept a second-class permanent membership. Japan had already taken a pro-veto position, saying that 'the new permanent members should be given the veto because without it they would be handicapped as members of the Council'.[19] However, in contrast to Japan, which believed that an assertive pro-veto stance might jeopardize its candidature at the time it was attempting to solicit support, Germany was not reluctant to complain.[20] Its permanent representative in the UN stated that it would not be fair for his country's permanent membership to be on an unequal footing with the other European permanent members. In 1994, the German diplomats in the UN did not mince their words when they said that

> the right of veto is *per se* not an objective for us. But our bottom line is clear: If Germany, as it was suggested, shall become a permanent member of the Security Council, this has to be on an equal footing with the other permanent members without discrimination, i.e. with the same rights and the same obligations. With respect to the existing European permanent members and in comparison to their status any different position for Germany could not be politically explained, let alone justified, *vis-a-vis* the public of our country which is the third largest contributor to the United Nations' budget.[21]

However, as the prospects of becoming permanent members became more favourable, Germany and Japan attempted to improve their credentials between 1993 and 1995. By 1995 the two countries had shouldered additional financial burdens and their contributions to the UN budget as well as to the budget for UN peacekeeping operations (PKO) rose significantly (see Tables 4.1 and 4.2). Thus, they made a strong connection between their financial contributions and the legitimacy of their candidature for permanent membership on the Council. As Japan pointed out, 'those countries that are clearly capable of assuming responsibility for the implementation of its resolutions by making financial contributions should be more actively involved in the decision-making process so as to ensure that the resolutions the Council adopts are in fact implemented.[22]

Germany and Japan had yet to decide whether or not they would commit their armed forces to major UN operations. They had eased their constitutional and legal restrictions to make this possible but both were still facing severe legal or political hurdles. On 15 June 1992, the Japanese Diet adopted a law that, while it allowed the so-called Self-Defence Forces to be used overseas as peacekeeping troops, did not permit Japan to take part in operations authorized by the Security Council under Chapter VII of the UN Charter.[23] In Germany, despite the Karlsruhe Constitutional Court's ruling of 12 July 1994, whereby it was declared that nothing in the Constitution prevented the use of German troops in UN missions, the

Table 4.1 Countries and percentage of contributions to the UN regular budget for 1995

Rank	Country	Percentage of contribution
1	United States	25.00
2	Japan	13.95
3	Germany	8.94
4	France	6.32
5	Russian Federation	5.68
6	United Kingdom	5.27
7	Italy	4.79
8	Canada	3.07
9	Spain	2.24
Others	China	0.72
	South Africa	0.34
	Nigeria	0.16
	Indonesia	0.14
	Egypt	0.07

Source: UN Doc. ST/ADM/SER.B/481, 8 December 1995, Status of Contributions as at 30 November 1995.

Table 4.2 Countries and percentage of contributions to the UN PKO budget for 1995

Rank	Country	Percentage of contribution
1	United States	31.15
2	Japan	14.05
3	Germany	8.97
4	France	7.87
5	Russian Federation	7.07
6	United Kingdom	6.56
7	Italy	4.81
8	Canada	3.08
9	Spain	2.25
10	Netherlands	1.58
Others	China	0.89
	South Africa	0.34
	Brazil	0.32
	Mexico	0.15
	India	0.06
	Nigeria	0.03
	Indonesia	0.02
	Egypt	0.01

Source: UN Department of Peacekeeping, New York, 1995.

government was facing difficulties in mustering sufficient public support 'for committing the Bundeswehr to distant, "out of area" operations where no strictly German interests were threatened'.[24]

Improving working practices as a means to diffuse pressure for substantial reform

Britain, France and the United States took advantage of this situation and sought recourse once again to obstructionism. By exposing Germany and Japan's inability to meet potential UN military obligations, they were trying to delay as long as possible the admission of the 'former enemies' to permanent membership. They were also buying time and hoping that other states would express opposition to the prospects of accepting an enlargement of the Council that included only Germany and Japan (the so-called quick fix formula).

Simultaneously, they exerted pressure on the Security Council to make moves in the direction of greater transparency and improvement in its working methods and procedures. They hoped that such moves might curb demands for changes in the Council's composition by states (other than Germany and Japan) that had persistently voiced concern over transparency in the work of the Security Council. By introducing changes in the working methods of the Council, the permanent members wanted to satisfy a large part of the UN membership and especially the group of non-aligned states who had criticized them for converting the Council into 'an incredibly hermetic' club.[25] The permanent members hoped that if this happened, it might lead a large number of states, not least the non-aligned states, to lift or at least moderate their demands for changes in the composition of the Council.

In fact, those who had been particularly offended by the Security Council's method of doing business were the non-aligned states. They had rightly complained that much of the real work of Council members used to take place away from the glare of publicity in the private meetings, sometimes of the three Western permanent members, sometimes of all five permanent members or in the informal consultations of the whole. Open public meetings, originally the principal means by which the Council conducted its business, had become more rare than the informal (or closed) meetings and, eventually, had lost their relevance. They were typically convened simply to endorse what had been agreed upon in private.

Realizing that efforts to restrict the closed meetings of the permanent members were bound to fail, the non-aligned states had focused much of their criticism on the informal consultations of the whole. They recognized the need to preserve informal consultations as a valuable mechanism for negotiation and compromise. But they had been concerned about two aspects of this practice: its secrecy, that is, the closed nature of these consultations during which no minutes or records of the topics discussed were kept, and the fact that these consultations were not open to non-members of the Council.[26] Thus, they had sought the institutionalization of the informal consultations of the whole through the Rules of Procedure of the Council and the incorporation in these Rules of a set of provisions, which would have made work in the informal consultations more transparent.[27] They had also underlined that the number of formal meetings of the Council had diminished in recent years (compared with the number of informal consultations of the whole).[28] For them informal consultations of the whole could be held whenever necessary, but not be used as the main way for the Council to conduct its business.

However, changes in the practice of informal consultations of the whole were not the only ones the non-aligned states had persistently demanded in order to see the Security Council take on more the characteristics of a glass house, with accessible and transparent procedures. They had also suggested a variety of measures aimed at improving the relationship of the Council with the member states.[29] Furthermore, they wished to strengthen the cooperation of the Council with the General Assembly and give real meaning to the political accountability of the former to the latter. Hence, they had recommended, *inter alia*, the institutionalization of the practice of regular consultations between the Presidents of the two organs on matters before the Council, 'with a view to keeping the Assembly apprised of developments in the Council which may be of interest to the general membership'.[30] They had also suggested that the Security Council should make more frequent, timely and analytical reports to the General Assembly. They also called on the UN membership to find additional ways and means to ensure that a steady and sufficient flow of information would be provided by the Security Council to the General Assembly, other organs of the UN and the regional agencies acting under Chapter VIII of the UN Charter.

A number of measures in this direction were adopted by the Security Council on the initiative or with the strong encouragement of the three Western permanent members in the period between 1993–5. The most important measures were the following:

1   Briefings of the President of the Council to non-members of the Council on the results of informal consultations of the whole.
2   Informal consultations of the whole and its provisional agenda to be announced, in advance in the *UN Journal*.
3   The monthly tentative forecast of work and the provisional agendas of the Council's upcoming (formal and informal) work to be provided monthly to all non-members of the Council, as are draft resolutions 'in blue' (i.e. in near-final form).
4   The procedures of the Sanctions committees to be made more transparent by the introduction of various new practices (such as increased use of press releases, quick preparation of summary records).

5   The decision to hold meetings between Council members, the Secretariat and members contributing troops to peacekeeping operations to facilitate exchanges of information prior to important Council decisions on peacekeeping operations.
6   The improvement of the format of the Security Council's reports to the General Assembly.[31]

These measures were welcomed by all UN members as 'noticeable developments',[32] which made the work of the Council more transparent.[33] But, while UN members and especially the group of the non-aligned states found these measures very useful, they asserted that they were a small proportion of those needed to bring the transparency and the functioning of the Council up to scratch. Apart from this, they complained that the implementation of the measures adopted was problematic in the sense that they had not been institutionalized yet. They were followed in practice but they had not been incorporated in the Rules of Procedure of the Security Council. Hence, their use had been at the mercy and the will of the Council and its President at any given time. The debate on further measures of transparency, they contended, should necessarily be part of the consideration of the wider issue of Council reform. But they proceeded to make clear that

> procedural reformulations in the working methods of the Council, meritorious as they may be, should not be taken as palliatives for a substantial restructuring of the Council itself. While more transparency may help to enhance its visibility, the effectiveness of the Council in discharging its responsibilities is more directly correlated to the adequacy of its structures for present realities and challenges.[34]

In essence, the member states of the UN, and especially the group of non-aligned states, sent an unequivocal message to the permanent members: that they were not prepared to accept measures of transparency, however laudable, as an alternative to or a substitute for Council reform.[35] In this way, they underlined the special importance they attached to the enlargement of the Council, aside from the question of transparency in the work of the Council. They also expressed their determination to play a more active role in the ongoing debate on Council reform.

The changing political context of the debate

Indeed, during the lengthy and exhaustive labours of the Open-Ended Working Group on Security Council Reform and the General Assembly that took place in 1995–6, most of the member states became actively involved in the debate. Their attitudes entirely changed the political context of the Council reform debate and shifted the focus away from

Germany and Japan to the search for a more broadly equitable representation on the Council. The majority of member states forwarded or supported reform proposals aimed at making the Security Council more representative of the UN as a whole, at augmenting the power of the countries of the South, and at reducing, through expansion of the Council and restrictions on the use of the veto, the perceived monopoly of power of the permanent five.

In the analysis that follows, the positions of the non-aligned states will be examined. The group consisted of 113 developing states, comprising virtually two-thirds of the UN membership and its power to influence UN reform should not be underestimated. The attitudes of the non-aligned states towards Council reform were important for two additional reasons: first, because they more or less reflected the interests and views of a majority of the UN membership and second, because their attitudes, along with those of certain European states, such as the Nordic countries, Spain and Italy (which will also be examined in the next section), were no doubt largely responsible for the changing political context of the debate on Council reform.

The non-aligned states

The political platform of the non-aligned states: No reform without us

Up until the end of 1994, deliberations in the UN reveal that the reform issue tended to be seen as an attempt by the permanent five to come to an agreement with Germany and Japan. However, the non-aligned states felt that, in discussions of the issue, the permanent five had been dismissive of their views, treating them as if they had no interest in the vital question of reform. These countries took action, therefore, to ensure that they would have a big say in any restructuring of the Council that would take place. Thus, in February 1995, the non-aligned states presented their own political platform for Council reform to the UN, stating that

> the non-aligned countries are grossly under-represented in the Council. This under-representation should, therefore, be corrected by the enlargement of the Security Council, which should enhance the credibility of the Council to reflect the universal character of the world body and to correct existing imbalances in the composition of the Security Council in a comprehensive manner.
>
> The extent, nature and the modalities of the expansion of the Security Council should be determined on the basis of the above principles [sovereign equality of states and equitable geographical distribution]. Attempts to exclude the Non-Aligned Movement from any enlargement in the membership of the Security Council would be

unacceptable to the movement.... If there is no agreement on other categories of membership, expansion should take place only, for the time being, in the non-permanent category.[36]

In putting forth their own platform, the non-aligned states were seeking (i) to articulate a different position from that of the permanent five, especially Britain, France and the United States, on the scope of the reform process and (ii) to warn the UN that they would not tolerate the debate on Council reform to continue in utter disregard of their views. Thus began an entirely new phase in the debate on Council reform.

The non-aligned states deliberately left their platform open in order to accommodate the variety of opinion that existed among them. Let's examine in some detail the different positions held by the non-aligned states on what they considered basic issues of Council reform: an increase in the number of permanent and non-permanent members, limitations in the scope and use of the veto as well as the improvement of the Council's working methods.

Permanent membership and related questions

While a majority of the non-aligned states were in favour of expanding permanent membership, they felt that there should be a corresponding increase in the number of non-permanent members so that the total membership of the Council be increased from 15 to 26 seats. This, of course, did not mean that they were prepared to accept the 'quick-fix' proposal of the United States, Britain and France, which would grant permanent membership status to Germany and Japan alone. The non-aligned states categorically rejected this proposal, arguing that any increase in the permanent membership of the Security Council that was limited to industrialized countries would not only aggravate the existing imbalance in the Council's membership but would also fail to acknowledge the increasing role played by developing states in promoting international peace and security. Representatives of many non-aligned nations in the UN made it clear that they would support the candidacies of Germany and Japan only if a few of their own were also granted permanent membership status. Since the admission of Germany and Japan to permanent membership would further tip the balance in favour of the industrialized states of the Northern hemisphere, the majority of the non-aligned states argued that it would be necessary to offset such an imbalance by including states from the Southern hemisphere.[37] As a Tunisian representative put it: 'Japan and Germany are claiming – understandably so – a permanent seat. These same realities entitle the developing countries to their proper place in the Council'.[38] Among those who sought an expansion in permanent members to include developing as well as developed states were important regional states such as Nigeria, Indonesia, India and South Africa. South Africa, for instance, stated that 'an increase in the permanent membership of the Security Council by the addition of countries from the developed world must be balanced by the addition of countries from the developing world'.[39]

A majority of the non-aligned states were in favour of a balanced increase in the permanent membership that included both developed and developing states, but when it came time to discuss the particulars of such expansion, they disagreed on a number of crucial issues. They were divided into two groups on questions of the scope of the expansion, the method of selection, and on whether to extend the right of veto to new members.

The first group, consisting of states mostly from Latin America and Asia, were in favour of the so-called 'two plus three' formula. This formula assigned two permanent seats to industrialized states (i.e. Germany and Japan), which, given their economic and political potential, had a real capacity to undertake global responsibilities, bolster the authority of the Council and shoulder a large part of the growing financial burden of the UN, while the other three permanent seats would be given to one country from each of the three southern regions, namely Africa, Asia and Latin America, including the Caribbean. Most of the supporters of the 'two plus three' formula agreed that the right of veto should not be granted to new permanent members. They believed that such an extension would only exacerbate an already undemocratic privilege which, they felt, in a post-Cold War world should actually be more restricted and, possibly, even abolished. In fact, what this group sought was a reform scheme, which, if implemented, would have led to the introduction of a two-tier structure of permanent membership with the existing permanent members retaining the right of veto while the newer permanent members would lack the veto power. This would have had the further effect of subdividing the Council's members into three categories: (i) current permanent members with the right of veto, (ii) permanent members without the veto (i.e. the five new permanent members), and (iii) non-permanent members. Of course, there were some non-aligned states who favoured the 'two plus three' formula but only if the right of veto were extended to the new permanent members. One of these states was India, which stated in the Open-Ended Working Group on Council reform that there should be no discrimination between the current permanent members and the new permanent members on the veto issue.[40]

As far as the method of selecting the five new permanent members was concerned, the proponents of the 'two plus three' formula came up with the so-called global selection method whereby the General Assembly would choose the new permanent members on the basis of objective criteria that they would formulate. India, for instance, stated that 'the choice of additional states to be selected for the permanent members' category should emerge from a decision of the General Assembly as provided in the Charter'.[41] With regard to the qualifications for the selection of regional permanent members, some of the proponents of the 'two plus three' formula questioned the necessity and timeliness of the discussion and elaboration of objective criteria at this juncture. They believed that this should be preceded by a decision on the expansion of the permanent membership itself by the UN members. However, others put forth their criteria for selecting the permanent members from the southern regions. India, for example, believed that consistency in support for and participation in important political and economic activities and peacekeeping operations of the UN and in fulfilling financial obligations should be the most important considerations in judging the suitability of a state that aspired to permanent membership.[42] Two other factors, India said, should also be taken into account: the population of the state and the size of its economy. Democratic states, with large populations, India believed, should be given increased rights of participation in international politics:

> population represents both an expression of the principle of democracy and an element of power. With increasing emphasis on the principle of democracy at the national level, there is a need for extending this principle to the international level also. The present permanent members of the Security Council have a combined population of less than 1.75 billion. This leaves two thirds of the world's population without representation in the permanent membership category.[43]

India also stressed the importance of the size, resiliency and self-sufficiency of the economy of a potential member, which, she pointed out, 'are factors that have a bearing on a particular country's ability to exercise independence of judgement and action on international issues'.[44] Indonesia agreed that population and economic potential, along with a capacity for exercising regional influence and lending support for UN peacekeeping activities, should be factors which deserved serious consideration in determining which states should become permanent members.[45] For the Central American countries of Costa Rica, El Salvador, Ecuador, Guatemala, Nicaragua[46] and Panama, the most important criteria were those already set forth in the UN Charter and which governed the election of non-permanent members.[47] For other states, such as the small states of the Caribbean Community,[48] the most important criterion was the ability and willingness to carry a large portion of the financial burden of the UN.[49] As countries with limited economic resources, they found their payments in support of UN peacekeeping activities quite burdensome. Thus, they made it clear that they would not oppose the idea of granting permanent seats to both developed and developing states that were economically capable of bearing a greater share of the UN's financial burden.[50] They hoped that in spreading the financial responsibilities to include the new permanent members, they would lessen their own financial burden.

The second group of non-aligned states wished to go beyond the 'two plus three' formula and proposed having more than three permanent seats for the developing states to redress the further imbalance that would come about should Germany and Japan be accepted as permanent members. Most of these were African states that found themselves in agreement with the position enunciated by the Council of Ministers of the OAU in 1994, which maintained that the representation of African states on the Security Council should be proportional to its membership in the UN and would entail Africa being assigned 'no fewer than two permanent seats'.[51] They justified their position by pointing out that Africa, with 53 members in the UN, had no permanent seat on the Council. South Africa,[52] Ghana,[53] Ethiopia,[54] Tunisia,[55] Tanzania,[56] Uganda,[57] Zimbabwe[58] and Kenya[59] were among those setting forth the common African position. Some of them also contended that not only Africa, but Asia and Latin America as well, should each have two permanent seats.

In contrast to the supporters of the 'two plus three' formula, almost all the African states that belonged to the NAM claimed that as long as the veto power was retained by the current permanent five it should be extended to all new permanent members as well. If not, they said, a new category of second-class permanent members would be created. African states such as South Africa and Uganda were voicing the common position of the members of the OAU. South Africa stated that the new permanent members should have all the rights and privileges associated with permanent membership.[60] Similarly, Uganda underlined that 'either the veto applies to all or it should be dispensed with'.[61] This point of view was also shared by some Arab states belonging to the NAM. Jordan, for instance, took the view that 'the permanent members whose addition is proposed must enjoy all the power of permanent membership laid down in the Charter, including the right of veto, because that, in our opinion, would bring about equitable representation as well as imposing a kind of cooperation between states, particularly, the permanent members'.[62]

As far as the method of selecting new permanent members was concerned, most African states preferred that of regional selection. They said that it should be up to the regions concerned to select the states to fill the new permanent seats.[63] Each region should devise its own method of selecting candidates based on characteristics. This meant that all new permanent seats to be allotted to developing states had first to be allocated to regions, which, in turn, would nominate the candidates for permanent membership in accordance with agreed-upon procedures. For their part, the African states claimed that two *rotating* permanent seats (with the right of veto) should 'be assigned to countries on the decision of the Africans themselves'.[64] As several African states emphasized, the two rotating permanent seats would belong to the region as a whole and thus the states occupying those seats would assume their responsibilities on the Council on behalf of the African continent. Those members sitting on the Council would thereby be accountable to the other African states with respect to how they discharged their mandate. As far as the other regions were concerned, it would be up to them to decide whether or not their permanent seats should be rotational.

A small number of non-aligned states, such as Chile[65] and Egypt,[66] questioned whether the inclusion of some developing states as permanent members was the best means of offsetting the imbalance that would result from the admission of Germany and Japan. For them, the most appropriate means of redressing the imbalance was by creating a new category of membership, so-called *semi-permanent* or *quasi-permanent* members, who would hover, so to speak, between permanent and non-permanent states. Their various proposals, although different in the details, agreed that these semi-permanent seats should be occupied by states that were representatives of the main regions of the developing world who would serve longer and/or more frequent terms than the existing non-permanent members. In effect, they were suggesting the subdivision of the Council into four categories: (1) current permanent members with the veto, (2) permanent members without the veto (i.e. Germany and Japan), (3) semi-permanent members without the veto, and (4) non-permanent members. As Egypt put it

> the Council should reflect both the nature and extent of the new balance of power, as well as the prominence of regional powers, with due regard to the interests of developing countries. It would therefore be beneficial to devise a new category of membership based on regional realities. An intermediary group of members between the permanent and the non-permanent ones should be established. One or more seats without veto power might be established for each region, to rotate between the major powers of that region.[67]

As previously stated, the overwhelming majority of the non-aligned states were in favour of an expansion in permanent membership. However, there was a bloc of some important non-aligned states, such as Pakistan, Argentina, Mexico, Colombia, Botswana, Libya, Sri Lanka and Lebanon, who opposed this reform entirely. They felt that there should be no changes in the current composition of permanent membership.[68] They called instead for a proportional increase only in the number of non-permanent seats. They would be happy to see the membership of the Council to be raised to 26 by the addition of 11 non-permanent seats.[69] The opponents of the expansion of the permanent membership argued that the enlargement of the non-permanent membership would contribute more substantially than an increase in permanent members to the democratization of the Council. They disagreed with the view that an increase in permanent members would lead to a more balanced and representative Security Council. They believed that an increase in the number of 'qualified' permanent seats, with or without the veto, would only serve the interests of these states and alienate the majority of others, thus exacerbating existing inequalities in the Council. In reality, the opposition to the idea of increasing the number of permanent seats arose out of the fear that the delegation of enormous prestige and influence of permanent membership to a single country in their respective regions would lead to the establishment of a regional hegemony of a single country over the entire region. Pakistan, for example, used this argument against the expansion of the permanent membership, saying that regional representation in the permanent membership would 'fuel the tendencies towards hegemony and domination which are manifest in some regions'.[70] This explains why the candidacies of some developing states for permanent membership, among them Brazil, India and Nigeria, had provoked criticism from their neighbours who would have been less than enthusiastic at the prospect. Argentina and Mexico, for instance, opposed Brazil and Pakistan opposed India. This bloc of states, which were against the idea of adding new 'qualified' permanent members, were also against the idea of introducing 'rotational permanent seats'. They asserted that if some states from the regions were to be given 'permanent seats' on a rotational basis, their attitude and voting behaviour in the Council would be influenced by their national perceptions of the issue at hand rather than by the perceptions of the regions they would be called on to represent.

Non-permanent membership and the size of the Security Council

All the non-aligned states were in favour of an increase in the number of non-permanent seats. Such an increase, they said, would help in redressing the imbalance between the size of the Council and the growth in UN membership. They also agreed that the criteria for selecting new non-permanent members should continue to be that stipulated in Article 23 (1) of the UN Charter, especially the 'equitable geographical distribution' criterion. They believed that this criterion, rather than that of 'contribution', should be the guiding principle for the expansion of the non-permanent membership in order to avoid unnecessary partiality and prejudice or regional imbalance. The overwhelming majority of the non-aligned states also agreed that the size of the Council should be increased from 15 to 26 seats.[71]

Limitations in the scope and use of the veto

Despite their deep divisions over the question of the expansion of the permanent membership of the Council, all the non-aligned members agreed that limitations on the scope and the use of the veto should be placed on both current and new permanent members. Realizing that those with the veto power would never consent to its abolition, the non-aligned states decided that the best option was to restrict its use by the permanent members as much as possible. Most of them regarded restriction as the first step towards abolition. This position was backed not only by those non-aligned states who supported the idea of adding new permanent members 'with all rights and responsibilities' (as expressed by representatives of the African states) but also by those who wanted enlargement to be limited to non-permanent members. Thus, many non-aligned states put forth suggestions for restrictions on the veto, which, in essence, amounted to a demand for changes in the existing voting system of the Security Council. They proposed to remove the use of the veto in: (1) decisions concerning the admission of new UN member states; (2) recommendations for the appointment of the UN Secretary-General; (3) decisions relating to provisional measures under Article 40 of the UN Charter; and (4) measures under Article 50 of the UN Charter relating to the economic problems of third countries arising from UN-imposed sanctions. Some of them went so far as to advocate that the veto should be restricted to decisions under Chapter VII of the Charter. There were also proposals for a change in the current voting system as outlined in Article 27 (3) of the Charter. Some of them, for example several African states, welcomed the idea put forward by the Netherlands by which two vetoes would be required to overturn a decision. In this way no one permanent member could unilaterally block the Council's decisions and recommendations. Others pointed to the fact that certain measures to limit the scope of the veto, being procedural in nature and to which the veto itself could not be applied, would not require an amendment of the Charter and could be made through revision of the Rules of Procedure of the Security Council.

The working methods of the Council

Changes in the Council's composition, the non-aligned states claimed, must be considered in tandem with a review of its working methods. The process of enlarging the Council, they pointed out, should be accompanied by a close scrutiny of the existing rules of procedure and by efforts to (i) increase the transparency and improve the functioning of the Council and (ii) address some of the tendencies and practices which run counter to fruitful cooperation between the Council and the whole membership of the UN. Although they realized that some progress in this direction had already been made in the years 1992–5, they deemed these measures not sufficient to make the work of the Council more transparent and more accessible to the UN membership. Thus, they tabled a comprehensive proposal that included all these measures which, in their viewpoint, could fully satisfy their demand for greater transparency in the work of the Council and more accountability of the Security Council to the general membership of the UN.[72]

The European states and others

In 1993–4, several European states, the Netherlands, Norway, Spain, Belgium and Croatia among them, took a position on Council reform that was slightly different from that of the United States, Britain and France. They felt that, besides the admission of Japan and Germany to permanent membership, there should be minor adjustments with regard to the number of non-permanent seats.

By the end of 1995 most of the European states participating in the debate had come up with proposals for Council reform that were significantly different from the 'quick-fix formula'. During discussions in the Open-Ended Working group and in the General Assembly, two informal groups of small and medium-size countries concluded that there was broad enough agreement between their positions on the main issues of Council reform to justify circulating papers and delivering speeches in the UN.

The first group consisted of Austria, Belgium, the Czech Republic, Estonia, Hungary, Ireland and Slovenia.[73] They proposed a Council of 20 to 25 members and an increase in permanent members by the addition of two or five seats. This, in essence, meant that they left open the possibility of supporting either the 'quick-fix' solution or the 'two plus three' formula (i.e. Germany and Japan, plus three developing states from Africa, Asia and Latin America). They also proposed that, in the selection of new permanent members, global influence and the capacity and willingness to contribute to international peace and security through peacekeeping operations and by assuming additional financial obligations should be taken into account. They avoided taking a clear position on the question of extending the veto to new permanent members but found merit in the proposals already made for its restriction in scope and application. They advocated an increase in the number of non-permanent seats to try to preserve a balance on the Council but they rejected the idea of semi-permanent or quasi-permanent members. Bulgaria, Croatia and Portugal took a similar position.

The second informal group consisted of the Nordic countries (Denmark, Finland, Iceland, Norway and Sweden).[74] They proposed a Council which would number 'in the low twenties, preferably 23'. They rejected the 'quick-fix' proposal and advocated the addition of five new permanent seats 'for qualified states'. In a number of position papers circulated in the UN between 1995 and 1997, the Nordic countries supported a 'two plus three permanent rotating' formula which, as it implies, would have granted permanent seats to Germany and Japan, while three 'regional rotating permanent seats' would have gone to developing states from Africa, Asia and Latin America. Regarding the procedure for selecting these three new permanent seats, the Nordic countries suggested that 'it would be for the countries in the regions to decide how the new permanent seats should be allocated. This could be to one single country; it could be to a few countries on a rotational basis; or it could be on another basis that the region might choose, the principle remaining that each region decide for itself'.[75] The General Assembly, they argued, should take into account any proposal by the regions concerned when making its final decision. By supporting the 'two plus three permanent rotating' formula, the Nordic countries came closer to the position of the African states. However, in contrast to the African states, the Nordic countries were concerned that an increase in the number of countries with the right of veto would not only harm the Security Council's decision-making process but would also diminish the role and influence of the non-permanent members on it.

The Nordic countries considered the non-permanent members to be an important part of the Council and believed that they should continue to constitute a clear majority on it. They proposed that a substantial number of the additional seats on an enlarged Council be set aside for elected non-permanent members. They also supported the idea that regional blocs should determine the rotation methods for non-permanent members and, to ensure maximum rotation, continue the ban on the immediate re-election of non-permanent members. Like the non-aligned states, they were in favour of restrictions on the use of the veto by the permanent members and called for changes in the working methods of the Council in order to achieve greater transparency.

A different position was taken by Spain, which sought a system allowing for more frequent rotation for the additional non-permanent seats on the Security Council.[76] Spain stopped short of saying how many additional non-permanent seats there should be. It simply advocated a system that would allow those states that were influential in international politics and had the capacity and determination to make a significant contribution to the UN to participate more frequently in the deliberations of the Council. These additional non-permanent members would serve longer terms than the existing non-permanent members would (i.e. more than two years). The regional groups would submit their candidates for the additional non-permanent seats to the General Assembly on the basis of three criteria: (1) extent of contribution of military, police and civilian personnel to UN peacekeeping operations, (2) amount of financial contribution to the UN budgets, and (3) the state's population as a percentage of the world's total. With regard to the third criterion, Spain stated that 'at a time when efforts are being made to democratize the Organization, it would be beneficial for the countries with larger populations to participate more frequently in the Security Council'.[77] Thus, a list of candidates would be drawn up and the General Assembly would choose from this list a certain number of states that would serve as non-permanent members.

In Spain's view, this proposal had three advantages: first, it would give those states which were not particularly rich or large an opportunity to be more frequently involved in the work of the Council; second, it would motivate some states to increase their military and financial contributions to the UN in order to become eligible for this special category of non-permanent membership; and third, the system was flexible and open enough so that any state could potentially meet the three criteria. As Spain saw it, the list of the additional non-permanent members could be renewed at the end of each cycle, allowing new states to be added on the basis of new calculations that reflected changes in participation in UN activities, contribution to the UN budgets and population. A similar proposal was presented by Turkey which suggested the addition of ten non-permanent seats to be chosen from a list of 30 or 40 states which could be renewed every 12 or 16 years.[78] However, neither Spain nor Turkey advocated an increase in the existing permanent or non-permanent membership of the Council.

Italy

Italy turned out to be one of the fiercest opponents of the 'quick-fix solution'. Its main argument was the same as that used by the non-aligned states, namely, 'the five current permanent members are all from the northern hemisphere, and almost all of them are fully industrialized. Adding two more with the same profile (i.e. Germany and Japan), rather than correcting this imbalance, would clearly aggravate it'.[79]

Italy attempted to convince the non-aligned states and the rest of the UN members that an increase in the number of permanent seats would lead to further inequality. Italian diplomats in the UN stated that the 'quick-fix formula' or the 'two plus three' proposal 'would benefit only two or five members of the United Nations, to the detriment of the remaining 175. The end result would be a small directorate of big countries, making critical decisions on questions that affect us all, but on which we would have no say'.[80] Such an increase, Paolo Fulci, the chief diplomat of Italy in the UN, argued, 'would double the number of Council members fully absolved from the need to stand for democratic election'.[81] Italy also reminded the small and medium-size countries that the current permanent members were assured of a continuing membership in other bodies of the UN (the so-called cascade effect) and that new permanent members would undoubtedly consider participation in these organizations an implicit and undeniable prerogative of their new status.[82] This would enable the permanent members – old and new – to take control over many bodies in the UN system. Moreover, Italy emphasized that the creation of additional permanent members in the Council was inextricably linked to the thorny question of the veto. Italy appealed especially to the non-aligned states who supported the expansion of the Council's permanent membership to attempt to persuade them that such a policy would (i) complicate the search for an enlargement of the Council because of disagreements over extending the veto to new members and of the potential difficulties with regard to the selection of the new members from the regions, and (ii) jeopardize the whole process of reform to the detriment of the majority of the UN members.

In 1995 Italy presented its own proposal,[83] which can be summarized as follows:

1   The current five permanent seats, along with their privileges, should remain unchanged. Apart from the existing ten non-permanent seats, a new class of eight or ten *rotating non-permanent seats* should be created. These new seats should be allocated on the basis of a geographical distribution formula, which 'should privilege the continents that are currently underrepresented'.[84] Specifically, Italy said that 'if ten new seats were added, five should go to Africa and Asia, two to the Latin American and the Caribbean states, two to the Western Europe and Others group, and one to Eastern Europe. In this way, 70 percent of the additional non-permanent seats would be reserved for developing countries'. Thus, Italy claimed, equitable rotation for every geographical group, to the advantage of all and not just of a few, would be ensured.

2   The additional non-permanent seats would rotate over a six-year period with each state being two years on and four years off the Council. This meant that for each of these new seats, three states would rotate, making a total of 24 or 30 states (i.e. 8 seats × 3 states or 10 seats × 3 states).

3   These new states would be selected by the General Assembly by a majority of two-thirds on the basis of objective criteria, such as contribution to the maintenance of international peace and security and to other purposes of the organization; capacity and willingness to contribute to peacekeeping operations with military personnel, equipment and financial resources; ability and willingness to participate in voluntary funds for humanitarian activities, economic development and the protection of human rights.

4   The list of the 24 or 30 countries would be subject to periodic review every 10, 12 or 15 years in order to avoid creating new possibilities of entrenched privilege. During these periodic reviews the General Assembly would assess which states had not honoured their responsibilities and commitments and replace them with other states more capable and willing.

5   No state on the list could compete for one of the regular ten non-permanent seats.

Italy's primary concern was, on the one hand, to ensure more frequent participation for itself on the Council and, on the other hand, to counter existing proposals such as the 'quick-fix solution' or the 'two plus three' formula or some other combination of increases in the permanent and non-permanent seats which would result, *inter alia*, in granting Germany a permanent seat on the Security Council.[85] The Italian proposal was carefully drafted to assure the realization of these objectives and sought to satisfy the different perspectives of the member states by incorporating basic elements from the proposals put forth by the Nordic countries, Spain and Turkey. It was also constructed to be consistent with the 'fall-back position' of the NAM countries which stated that, should it prove to be impossible to reach an agreement on an increase in permanent membership, there should be an increase, for the time being, only in non-permanent seats. Generally speaking, the Italian proposal was designed to be attractive to the majority of the UN members, especially to the small and middle-size states, most of whom belonged to the NAM. The proposal allowed for increased representation in the new class of non-permanent members of a number of non-aligned states thereby increasing their participation in the decision-making process of the Council. Furthermore, since the proposal made the rotating non-permanent members ineligible for the ten seats occupied by the non-permanent members, the small and medium-size states, which composed the bulk of the UN membership, would be given a fairer chance of being elected more often to a non-permanent seat. These states would no longer have to compete with their larger neighbours, who systematically elbowed them out at every turn in the election process. As Italy put it: 'those who would benefit the most from our proposal would be the smaller and mid-sized states'. In order to make its arguments more convincing, Italy presented to the members of the Open-Ended Working Group a table which showed that, from 1946 to 1995, 79 small and mid-sized states had not served on the Council, while 43 had served only once.[86] Despite its similarities to the Spanish and Turkish proposals, the Italian plan was intended to meet the demands better of a large part of the UN membership for an equitable representation in the composition of the Council of all the geographical groups without any numerical discrimination.

Thus, the Italian proposal caught the member states' attention. As pointed out by David Malone, former Deputy Permanent Representative of Canada in the UN, the specifics of the Italian proposal 'put a very energetic cat amongst the pigeons'.[87] Support grew steadily for the Italian proposal while at the same time there was a noticeable decline in support for the 'two plus three' formula or its variants (e.g. the two + more than three permanent seats for developing states or the two plus a number of regional permanent rotating seats), all of which meant an increase in the number of permanent seats. By early 1996, a large number of states (Italy claimed 58 adherents) had expressed support for or interest in the major elements of the Italian proposal or saw it as a potential 'fall-back formula' in the likely event that agreement on an increase in the permanent membership could not be reached. Among them were important states like Egypt, Ukraine,[88] Australia and Canada,[89] which found that the Italian proposal, especially the provision for the creation of an additional class of non-permanent seats, suited them quite well. For instance, Egypt, a leading member of the NAM, thought that the Italian proposal should be carefully studied because it was consistent with the 'fall-back formula' of the NAM. Egypt outlined its position:

> [I]t must be admitted that the creation of additional permanent seats in the Council runs into two obstacles that are not easily surmountable. The first relates to the negative effects on the work of the Council that would result from increasing the number of members with the right of veto. The second concerns the many difficulties which stand in the way of reaching agreement on third-world states that would be given permanent seats in the Council, especially in view of the diversity of situations, characteristics and political circumstances in Asia, Africa and Latin America. In view of all this, it would be more to the point, both in terms of logic and practical terms, to focus, in the next phase, on exploring the range of ideas submitted by certain states such as Italy, on developing a new method for selecting certain states on the basis of their regional weight and on giving them special responsibilities...[90]

A similar view was expressed by Australia:

> [W]e believe that the Working Group must concentrate on working out a modality for non-permanent expansion that would be acceptable to the general membership, rather than focusing on a highly divisive and controversial issue, namely, whether or not permanent members should be added. In this connection, I agree with the views of the Italian Ambassador that we stand at the crossroads, leading either to new permanent seats or to new elected seats, and I emphasize, elected seats.[91]

The Italian proposal was also supported by states that, from the start of the debate on Council reform, had made it clear that they would support an increase only in non-permanent membership. It was also backed by small states, such as Malta,[92] San Marino,[93] the Republic of Korea[94] and Venezuela,[95] which believed (for the reasons discussed above) that the Italian proposal would, in effect, offer the small member states the opportunity as non-permanent members to be elected more often. As expected, states like Spain[96] and Turkey[97] were also favourably disposed to the Italian proposal because it embodied the basic elements of the proposals of the Open-Ended Working Group. It is worth noting at this point that several states, which supported the Italian proposal, felt the Spanish and the Turkish proposals worthy of consideration because, like the Italian formula, they offered the possibility of having some member states serving more frequently, but not permanently, on the Security Council.

5   The debate in the UN: 1996–2000

The changing attitude of the permanent members

As was discussed in the previous chapter, the scenario for an enlargement of the Security Council that would include only Germany and Japan (the quick-fix formula) had been receding in the course of the debate that took place in the period 1994–6. This scenario was declared off the negotiating table as it was made clear that it could not attract the support it needed to be a realistic option. In recognition of this reality, the 1995–6 report of the Open-Ended Working Group explicitly stated that 'in the event that there is agreement for an increase in the permanent membership, an increase only by industrialized countries would be widely regarded as unacceptable'.[1]

In addition, it became clear that the implementation of any of the Council reform proposals which were floated, discussed or supported by member states during this period would have serious repercussions for the permanent five. First, expanding the number of permanent members of the Security Council would shift the balance of power and dilute the permanent five's special status at the core of the group of the most influential states in the world. Second, proposals such as those supported by the members of the non-aligned group or Italy, which sought an increase of the total number of Council members to 26 and 24, respectively, if adopted, would put the power of the permanent five – that is their ability to determine outcomes – at stake. The addition of 10 or 11 new seats would mean that it would become more difficult for any one of the permanent five to get a controversial or a strong resolution adopted, because more votes would now be needed. Under these circumstances individual permanent members, like Russia or China, would lose political weight, as they did not have the power possessed by the United States, as the sole superpower, 'to persuade other members of the Council to vote with it from common principles of ideology, or through rewards of side payments, or by implicit threats of punishment'.[2] Furthermore, a broad Council expansion might activate the so-called informal veto, that is, the capacity of a group of states other than the veto-wielding permanent members to prevent decisions from being taken.

Finally, the most important proposals that were presented during this period would, if adopted, materially diminish the importance of the veto power in that they included demands for restricting in one way or another its use by the permanent five. All these proposals included provisions that would severely limit the scope and the use of veto, while some of them provided that two or three negative votes by permanent members should be required for a veto to take effect. Considering the significance of the veto as an instrument of policy, any dilution of the power of veto implied that the permanent five would be surrendering a major source of their international influence and strength. The veto continued to be the weapon that the permanent five could use as a last resort in order to prevent the adoption of resolutions that were contrary to their national interests. For each of the current permanent members there was clearly a correlation between the value of the veto and the degree of their isolation on substantive issues. This was particularly true for permanent members such as Russia or China, which did not have 'natural allies' within the club of permanent members on whose support they could count every time their national interests were at stake. Apart from that, for permanent members, such as Britain and France, the veto had become a crucial instrument for remaining global players and for influencing international developments. Through their veto, they could ensure that despite the loss of their great power status and the subsequent loss of prestige, they could exert some level of control on the outcome of international affairs. For them, as for post-Soviet Russia, which had lost its superpower status, the veto represented a coveted 'prize', which was inextricably linked to their position of permanent membership of the Security Council; any challenge to their veto power would be inconceivable.

In the light of the new developments, all permanent members except China were compelled to modify their attitude towards reform of the Security Council. Thus, it was deemed necessary to work out a strategy, which would acknowledge the international impetus for reform whilst allowing for the least possible changes in the status quo.

First, Britain, Russia and the United States publicly accepted that they could no longer contain expansion of permanent membership to only two new members and came out in support of the 'two plus three' formula, whereby three out of five permanent seats would go to developing countries. Russia, for instance, declared that 'Germany and Japan are real candidates for a reformed Council. It is also clear, however, that the attainment of a broad agreement with regard to the parameters of the expanding Council implies the granting of permanent seats to representatives of Asia, Africa and Latin America'.[3] The three permanent members explicitly told the Open-Ended Working Group on Council Reform and the General Assembly that they were unwilling to discuss any increase beyond 20 or 21 Council members in total.[4] This meant that they were not prepared to accept an expansion in the non-permanent membership. They made clear that they considered it crucial to maintain a compact and operational Security Council membership and that exceeding the quantitative limit of 20 or 21 would have, as they pointed out, a negative impact on the efficiency of the Security Council's activities. 'It is not a search for a magical number but rather of ensuring real efficiency of the Council. We must not turn the Council into a "discussion club", the Russians said.[5] The permanent three tried to justify their position arguing that the Security Council should remain organized on the principles of responsibility and efficiency, rather than on the principle of democratic representation. As they pointed out, the challenge would be to achieve the difficult balance whereby membership of the Security Council would reflect current global power relationships but not be so large as to make it an unwieldy body. But there was one more reason that made the three express strong opposition to an increase in the number of non-permanent members: they wanted to exclude the possibility of the developing states (by their permanent and non-permanent seats) creating a solid bloc and exercising an effective 'group veto' (the so-called sixth veto). France distanced itself from the position of the permanent three, saying that it was not against the idea of increasing slightly the number of non-permanent seats. As it explicitly stated, 'we are in favour of admitting Germany and Japan, as well as three countries of the South to permanent membership [i.e. the 'two plus three' formula] and support the creation of new non-permanent seats in order to improve the Council's geographical representation'.[6] It maintained that the total number of members should remain below 25.

China had been the least specific of all the permanent members in that it had not mentioned any specific number of new seats that should be added to the Council. Its Permanent Representative to the UN called for a reform of the Council, which must

> focus on redressing imbalanced regional representation, particularly serious inadequacy in the representation of developing states. It must in no way further aggravate such imbalance. Without attaining this objective, the enlargement of the Council cannot be regarded as reform in the real sense, but rather a failure of the reform. Therefore, no reform plan that excludes or discriminates against developing countries will ever be accepted by the general membership of the UN, including China.[7]

The problem with this ostensibly open-minded position was the absence of clarity as to whether China would be prepared to see developed and/or developing states being given permanent seats. However, developing states were a little comforted by the fact that China repeatedly referred to the need for what it called 'broadening participation in the Council by developing states'. But, of course, this was not exactly the same thing as clearly supporting permanent seats for developing states.

Second, all of the permanent five explicitly declared that they would oppose any limitations to their own veto right. The United States, Britain and Russia were the most vocal among the permanent five in refuting the proposals for abolishing or restricting the exercise of the veto.[8] Interfurth, the American Ambassador to the UN, stated in the Open-Ended Working Group on Security Council Reform that his country was firmly opposed to any attempt to restrict or curtail the veto, be it through amendment to the Charter or in any other way.[9] Sir Weston, the British Permanent Representative to the UN, also made it clear that his country was not going to support any abridgement of the right of veto or its scope of application. It is worth quoting his statement in full:

> the veto power is popularly associated with the period of the Cold War when the Council was largely unable to function in major confrontations between the two major blocs. The existence of the veto at least protected the authority of the United Nations from being co-opted or usurped by one bloc or the other. The role of the United Nations may have been diminished during the Cold War but a consequence of the veto in those years was that the United Nations survived, and that the organization has become the forum for genuine cooperation between the members of the same blocs since the end of the Cold War. While we see no likelihood of a return to international bloc politics, the fact that the veto served in those years to protect the neutrality of the United Nations and its unique position as the single global forum accepted by all is still relevant.[10]

Likewise, Russia clearly communicated its intention to defend the fully fledged right of veto of the permanent five. Its Permanent Representatives to the UN expressed this uncompromising stand on many occasions, stating that

> any restriction of the status enjoyed by the current permanent members of the Security Council is unacceptable, including ideas of curtailing the institution of the veto in all its forms. That is one of the most vital conditions for a feasible resolution of the issue of enlargement of the Security Council. The issue has a strong resonance in Russian domestic politics, given that it is to be submitted to the state Duma for its ratification and will be followed by public and political reverberations throughout the country.[11]

The Russian chief diplomats argued further that they did not share the opinion held by some other delegations that the right of veto was an anachronism inherited by the UN from the times of the Cold War. Echoing the British position, Russia claimed that the veto right was an instrument that ensured unity among the great powers. It perceived the veto as an 'in-built stabilizer' of the UN and 'a critically important and indispensable component of the mechanism of harmonizing positions and decision-making in the Council'. 'The disintegration of this integral mechanism', the Russians warned, 'is likely to hamper the Security Council's ability to work'.[12]

The permanent five were opposed to any change in their veto right but did not take a position on the question of extending the veto to new permanent members. As they stated, they saw no point in further discussions of this matter, because the existing insurmountable differences in the approaches of member states to the question of veto impeded their ability to reach an agreement on the issue of Council expansion. Thus, they fudged the issue of veto by insisting that the debate on offering the veto to new permanent members be postponed until after they had taken their seats.[13] In this way, they tried to divorce the issue of the expansion of Council membership from the issue of the veto. This of course contradicted repeated calls by the member states that the issues in the reform package should be considered as an integrated whole.

Britain, Russia and the United States had distilled the maze of arguments and proposals that had been put forward during the course of the discussions and promoted what they considered the least damaging proposal for change. In short, they accepted the 'two plus three' formula instead of only Germany and Japan, agreed to an increase of the total Council membership to a maximum 20 members, but categorically rejected the proposals for an increase in the non-permanent membership and any notion of reform of the veto. This position was dictated by their need to present a reform plan which would keep change to a minimum and would thus have less of a negative impact on (i) their status as permanent members and their capacity to influence decisions in that body and (ii) the principle of great power cooperation, in the absence of which the Security Council could not function effectively. They also appeared to believe that since their proposal would, in effect, increase developing countries representation in the category of permanent membership, it would satisfy the positions of a large number of member states. It would also help the permanent members to redress criticism that the Security Council was made up solely of rich industrialized states.

As a matter of fact, the revised attitude of the permanent members toward Council reform had a double effect on the discussions: (i) it confounded further the candidacies of Germany and Japan and (ii) made the reform process more complicated than ever. By supporting the admission of Germany, Japan and three developing states to the Security Council's permanent membership, Russia, the United States, France and Britain put obstacles in the way of the German and Japanese case for acquiring, if accepted as permanent members, equal rights with the current permanent five.[14] At least half of the non-aligned states and a large number of other states, most of them from Europe, had been against the idea of granting the right of veto to any new permanent members. This meant that

Germany's and Japan's request for permanent seats accompanied by the right of veto had little chance of success if it ever came to a vote. These two states could hardly command the required support of two-thirds of the UN membership.

Furthermore, since four of the five permanent members linked Germany's and Japan's candidacies to those of three developing states, Japan and Germany had now to wait for the developing states to agree to a common position on representation for permanent membership in the Council. This was a highly complex task for the developing states. As was seen in the previous chapter, there was serious divergence among the developing states on a number of crucial questions pertinent to the expansion of the permanent membership. There were still differing views among them on the need to expand the permanent membership, and on the modalities and criteria for the selection of possible new members. There was also a disparity among the various views on the question of the extension of veto to new permanent members. Furthermore, even if the developing states were to agree on the 'two plus three' formula and on all issues relevant to the expansion of the permanent membership, a long distance had to be covered in order to reconcile the views of the developing states with those of the current permanent members on the question of the total size of the Council. The former favoured an increase to 26 seats, while the latter, being opposed to the idea of enlarging the non-permanent membership of the Council, were prepared to accept only a limited increase to 20 seats. In the light of these problems, in 1997, Ambassador Ismael Razali of Malaysia attempted to put forward a compromise solution, the so-called Razali plan which, up until this time, constituted the single most important and most coherent reform proposal. Although it proved to be unworkable, it demonstrated the complexities, conflicting interests and shortcomings surrounding Security Council reform.

The Razali plan: a solution to the deadlock?

On 20 March 1997, the then President of the General Assembly, Ambassador Ismael Razali of Malaysia, outlined before the Open-Ended Working Group a reform plan aimed at breaking the deadlock on Security Council reform after more than three years of discussions. Razali believed that his initiative could result in a swift conclusion to the negotiating process. 'The Open-Ended Working Group', he said, 'should not be seen as a place for endless talk – that would give the United Nations a bad image'.[15]

Razali introduced a three-stage reform plan.[16] According to the plan, in the first stage between June and September, the General Assembly should vote a resolution calling for the Security Council to be enlarged to include five new permanent members (two from industrialized and three from developing countries with one each from Africa, Asia, and Latin America and the Caribbean) and four non-permanent members. The four non-permanent members would come from Africa, Asia, Eastern Europe, and Latin America and the Caribbean). In the second stage, the Assembly would pass, by 28 February 1998, a second resolution that would fill in the blanks by selecting specific candidate states. It was understood that, although Germany and Japan were not mentioned by name, it was they that Razali had in mind when he referred to the 'two industrialized' countries that should enter as permanent members. Both resolutions would be put to vote in accordance with Article 18 of the Charter for 'important questions', that is by two-thirds majority of Assembly members *present and voting*. As was provided in the Razali plan, if the number of states having obtained the required majority fell short of the number of seats allocated for permanent membership, new rounds of balloting would be conducted for the remaining category or categories, until five states obtained the required majority to occupy the five seats. In the third stage the Assembly would, no later than one week following designation of the states to be elected to serve as new Council members, vote on a resolution implementing the two previous resolutions as Charter amendments. This resolution would need to be approved by two-thirds of all member states as stipulated in Article 108. The third resolution would include amendments to Article 27 (2) and (3) of the UN Charter requiring the affirmative vote of 15 of 24 members of the Security Council for decisions.

The Razali plan also provided that for peacekeeping assessments, all new and old permanent members would undertake to pay the same percentage rate of premium surcharge over and above their regular budget rate of assessment. Razali proposed that the five new permanent members would not have veto power while the current five holding the veto would be encouraged to limit its use to actions under Chapter VII of the UN Charter which provides for enforcement measures. He invoked the principle of inequity in order to explain to the members of the Open-Ended Working Group on Council Reform why he was against the idea of extending the right of veto to new permanent members. He argued that

> I find it inconsistent and unacceptable both logically and morally to extend such a power [i.e. the veto power] to new permanent members of the Security Council. To do so would be to compound an inequity. The incoming five new permanent members are different: They are elected and have not inherited their powers or their membership as a result of 1945. It is my belief that concepts of the functions and responsibilities of permanent membership of the Security Council must begin to evolve so that it is de-coupled from, or no longer equated with, the possession of the veto power.[17]

The Razali plan also called on the Security Council to adopt a series of modifications in its working methods and procedures along the lines suggested by the members of the non-aligned group and other states.

Ambassador Razali, in his capacity as Chairman of the General Assembly and of the Open-Ended Working Group, came up with a comprehensive package of proposals for moving the reform process forward. He believed that his plan reflected the mainstream current in the debate. The package, which was conceived and put together from a pragmatic standpoint, represented the negotiating middle ground. Whatever the diversity of views among its supporters or opponents, it offered by far the best prospect for a solution thus far because it attempted to reconcile the views of the greatest possible number of states. The challenge for the member states was really to work on the basis of the spirit of compromise and an underlying political will to make progress towards achieving a fair and credible reform of the Security Council.

The attitude of UN members toward the Razali plan

The reaction of the five permanent members to the Razali plan varied. Most Western powers reacted somewhat reservedly to the plan. Bill Richardson, the American chief diplomat at the UN, welcomed the plan's idea for a stage-by-stage approach and the procedure outlined in the Razali plan (i.e. the adoption by the General Assembly of three resolutions under different voting requirements). He also made clear that his government continued to agree in principle to having Germany and Japan as well as three named or rotational developing states sit on the Council. But he reiterated Washington's opposition to any Council membership increase to more than 20 or 21 states. In a statement he made to the Open-Ended Working Group, he underlined that 'we have no flexibility above and beyond 20–21 seats on a reformed Council. This would permit expansion of the Council by one-third, with up to five new permanent members'.[18] By giving to the other members of the Open-Ended Working Group a warning that the United States 'would oppose any resolution which called for higher numbers', Richardson wanted to say that his country was reluctant to accept the Razali plan, at least in its present form, as a basis for negotiations. Russia took a similar position. In fact, the central elements of the positions taken by the United States and Russia made it unlikely that progress could be made, except on the basis of the submission of all other UN members to the American and Russian wishes. Britain and China avoided taking positions on the merits of the Razali plan but, like the other permanent members, expressed serious reservations regarding the rigorous schedule of the plan. Of all the permanent members, France was the only one that welcomed the Razali plan. It saw the plan as an opportunity to begin in earnest the process leading to expansion of the Council.[19] As France stated 'the approach proposed by President Razali entails proceeding in several stages. This approach has the advantage of allowing sufficient time for agreement to emerge gradually, first on a framework and then on the names of the new members'.[20]

The Razali plan caused serious divisions among the rest of the UN membership. There was a bloc of states that saw the plan as the proposal that could bring the hitherto fruitless discussions to an end. Among them were Germany, Japan, Brazil and India who believed that the Razali plan would offer them the chance to realize their ambition to become permanent members. Japan and Germany hailed the proposal as a realistic plan, which successfully compromised conflicting points of view. Both candidates had now come to realize that in order to buy backing from the developing states for their bid for permanent membership, they had to accept the inclusion of some of them in both permanent and non-permanent categories. Both wanted to show flexibility in the ensuing talks and deliberately played down the importance of the veto issue. Of course, they did not neglect to express disappointment that the Razali plan would withhold a veto from the incoming permanent members. But for tactical reasons they appeared reluctant to burden the early stage of the negotiations on the Razali plan with such a divisive issue. In all likelihood, they would raise the issue later. Germany only criticized the Razali plan for envisaging an action-threshold (15 affirmative votes), which was 'rather high'. As it stated 'it may hamper taking difficult decisions and therefore should be lowered'.[21] Support for the Razali plan was also expressed by the majority of Central and Eastern European states because it would ensure one additional non-permanent seat for their region where the number of states had more than doubled in recent years. The Nordic countries and other European countries such as Belgium, Austria, the Netherlands, and Portugal indicated that the reform proposal of Razali had advanced the reform process and did provide a plausible framework enabling states to start concrete negotiations leading to a general agreement.

NAM 'kills' the Razali plan but saves its unity

The Razali plan would have, if adopted, significantly increased the participation of non-aligned states in the Council, thus allowing them to have a significant voice in its decision-making and, by implication, to the UN as a whole. But the overwhelming majority of NAM countries chose not to associate themselves with it.

The main question that arises is why NAM countries rejected outright the Razali plan instead of suggesting changes in its content? The answer to this question is that the NAM felt that its very existence was at stake. It could not sacrifice the unity of the Movement just to ensure a number of seats for some of its members in the Council. The Movement perceived that since its members were still deeply divided on the basic issues of reform, they would be unlikely to take a common stand in favour of the Razali plan. It also believed that it would be very risky to allow its members the freedom to take their own decisions on the merits of the plan. If that were the case, it was very probable that a number of non-aligned states would express support for the plan. Were the Razali plan adopted, it would have resulted in the elevation of a few developing states to permanent membership. This, given the serious rift among the NAM members on the issue of enlargement of the permanent members and that they had been unable to agree on unified nominations, would have serious repercussions for the unity of the Movement. It would have brought further discord within its ranks, disrupting and undermining its very purpose, namely to generate among its members common interests and internal loyalties which would enable it to establish a common front with regard to crucial issues arising on the international scene. The NAM could assert itself as the collective spokesman for the developing world and have an influence on world affairs including those dealt with in the context of the UN, only if its members were able to display a high degree of unity and cohesion. The NAM considered that the Razali plan would put the viability of the Movement under severe strain. Thus, it felt that for its own survival, it had to tie its members down to an agreement not to go ahead with the plan.

In the light of the seriousness of the problem facing the NAM, the Ministers for Foreign Affairs of the non-aligned states met twice, in New Delhi on 7 and 8 April and in New York on 25 September 1997. One of the chief tasks of the Ministers at these meetings was to coordinate their efforts and establish guidelines to enable the members of NAM to work in a collective manner on issues regarding restructuring of the UN, not least on the issue of Security Council reform. The Ministers reviewed discussions, which had taken place in the Open-Ended Working Group on Council reform and realized that important differences still existed among them on a number of issues of reform, including the Razali plan. In the ensuing declarations of the two meetings, the Ministers of Foreign Affairs of the non-aligned states underlined 'the necessity of the Movement [i.e. NAM] maintaining its unity and solidarity on this critical issue'.[22] They also stated that the Movement should, in the subsequent negotiations, be guided by the following considerations in approaching the issue of Security Council reform in discussions at the UN:

1   that both reform and expansion of the Security Council should be considered as an integral part of a common package;
2   that the under-representation of the developing states should be corrected by enlargement of the Council in order to correct existing imbalances in its composition;
3   that attempts to exclude NAM from any Council enlargement would be unacceptable to the NAM;
4   that the membership of the Council should be increased by not less than 11 members;
5   that the negotiating process should be truly democratic and transparent;

6   that efforts at reforming the Security Council shall not be subject to any imposed time frame. No effort should be made to decide Council reform before general agreement is reached;

7   that if there is no agreement on other categories of membership, expansion should take place only, for the time being, in the non-permanent category;

8   that the veto should be curtailed with a view to its elimination and that the UN Charter should be amended so that, as a first step, the veto power should only apply to actions under Chapter VII of the UN Charter;

9   that any resolution with Charter amendment implications should faithfully comply with the provisions of Article 108 of the UN Charter.

In fact, a number of the directives NAM members were called upon to pursue in the negotiations on Council reform were not new. They had been elaborated in previous meetings of NAM and had been contained in the position paper adopted by the Movement on 13 February 1995. There were, however, some new directives given by the two ministerial meetings of NAM in 1997, which indicated to the non-aligned states which approach they had to follow with regard to the Razali plan. Directives 4 to 9 although not explicitly mentioning the Razali plan, conveyed to the non-aligned states the mandate to coordinate their positions in the UN with a view to rejecting it. Uppermost in the minds of NAM was that it had to save the unity of its members, even though the price was effectively to 'kill' the Razali plan and, consequently, dash all their hopes for a greater role in the decision-making mechanism of the Council. What was more at stake at this crucial moment for the NAM was its existence, which hinged upon the unity and cohesion of its members, the Ministers of Foreign Affairs of non-aligned states proclaimed.[23]

Fully committed to the directives given by the two ministerial meetings of the NAM held at New Delhi and New York, the overwhelming majority of non-aligned states launched a severe attack against Razali himself and his plan. They were unwilling to recommend changes to the proposed plan because they wanted to treat it as an 'all or nothing proposition', thus leaving no room for negotiations. Among the most militant against the Razali plan were states, such as Pakistan, Indonesia, Argentina and Mexico, which would not like to see their regional rivals elevated to permanent membership and other regional powers, such as Egypt or Indonesia, which were unlikely to win permanent seats.

Without being able themselves to present an alternative reform proposal, the non-aligned states accused Razali, the Permanent Representative of Malaysia, of producing this plan with no mandate from the Open-Ended Working Group. They pointed out that the Chairman, acting in his capacity as Chairman of the Open-Ended Working Group, may act to give impulse to the debate and revive it, but that his role should stop there. The Chairman must avoid the temptation of taking part in the game. There was general discontent among the non-aligned states with Razali's 'extra-ordinary' initiative which, as the non-aligned states said, threatened to overtake the debate of the Working Group itself. This discontent was expressed by remarks such as those of Pakistan. Its permanent Representative to the UN stated emphatically that

> it is true that each one of us can dream of trysts with history, and come forward with visionary ideas and suggestions. But we do so in all cases as representatives of our respective countries, and not as the representatives of the Working Group as a whole. So if your paper comes from the Permanent Representative of Malaysia, we would have no quarrel with it, but if it carries the stamp of the Chairman, then it clearly gives the impression that it was asked by all of us, or that we stand behind it, which is not the case. The powers of the General Assembly, and of the Chairmen of the Working Groups, are defined by Rules 35 and 36 of the Rules of Procedure, and do not confer '*suo moto*' powers as are given to the Secretary-General under Article 99 of the Charter.[24]

The Razali plan came under harsh criticism in both the Open-Ended Working Group on Council reform and in the General Assembly, as the elements of the plan did not correspond to the positions of NAM countries. Razali, the non-aligned states complained, dropped 'a bombshell on 20 March 1997, by putting forward his own paper'.[25]

They argued that it was wrongly labelled as representing the 'main-stream view' and that while the NAM, comprising 113 states, had demanded an expansion of the total size of the Council from 15 to 26, Razali claimed that the mainstream supported the lower figure of just 24. They also doubted Razali's view that the 'two plus three' formula for permanent membership, which was embodied in his plan, had 'main-stream' support and, in addition, underlined that the demand of the African states to have two rotational seats in the category of permanent membership with the same prerogatives as the existing permanent members had been ignored. This view was particularly supported by the African state members of NAM including Egypt. The latter hoped that the allocation of two permanent seats to the African region would increase its chance to be elected as a permanent member, 'geographically representing the northeastern sub-region of Africa and politically representing the Arab population'.[26]

The initiative of Razali to table his own proposal was seen by the non-aligned states as an attempt to gloss over the deep differences on core issues and to push the process forward artificially. For them, owing to the existing differences, basic issues of Council reform could not be subjected

or negotiated according to any predetermined timetable. But the most dis-
turbing aspect of his plan was the proposal to expand the Council in three
stages. They complained that the stage-by-stage approach did not have the
support of the mainstream, as it had never been discussed in the Open-
Ended Working Group, and that it was deliberately introduced to circumvent the provisions of the UN Charter relating to Charter amendment. As
already mentioned, the plan envisaged a three-stage Council enlargement:
first, a *framework* resolution increasing the number of permanent and
non-permanent members; second, an *implementing* resolution selecting the
new permanent members; and third, a *conceptual* resolution formally
amending the Charter. According to the proposal, only the last resolution
would have to be approved by a two-thirds majority of all member states
(Article 108), while for the previous two resolutions, a two-thirds majority
of Assembly members *present and voting* would suffice (Article 18).

According to the non-aligned states the plan was 'a constitutional
absurdity', since new permanent seats could be established and new
permanent members selected with less votes than those required for
Charter amendment. Any reform of the Council must be effected by the
largest majority provided for in the UN Charter, as set forth in Article 108
(at least 124 states). Many non-aligned states underscored the fact that the
provisions of Article 108 were a safety net, in that the application of
Article 18 could lead to the possibility of resolutions being adopted by a
small number of positive votes, a number which could well represent less
than half of the UN members. This result would not be commensurate
with the importance of issues involving the amendment of the Charter's
provisions, they argued. The non-aligned states reminded the members of
the UN that the 1963 enlargement of the Council from 11 to 15 members
adding four new non-permanent members had been effected in a manner
consistent with the constitutional requirements stipulated for Charter
amendments. At the time, the General Assembly had voted on a single resolution (i.e. Resolution 1991A of 17 December 1963) in accordance with
Article 108. A large number of non-aligned states explicitly warned that
any amendment resolution not adopted by the majority stipulated in
Article 108 '[w]ould fail to meet the test of legitimacy'.[27] For the General
Assembly to consider adopting under Article 18 a resolution in respect of
Security Council enlargement which had UN Charter amendment implications would do grave damage not only to the 1963 precedent but also to
the Charter itself. As they put it, the procedure established in Article 108
was clearly intended by those who drafted the Charter to apply to
decisions with Charter amendment implications, which are distinct from
those kinds of important questions contemplated by Article 18. The discussions on reform are about fundamental changes to the structure of the
most important organ of the UN, the non-aligned states underlined.

The members of NAM used the plan's legal ambiguity to argue that it
was a device intended to let specific states like Germany and Japan sneak

into permanent seats through the back door. As chief diplomats of non-aligned states pointed out, '[a]ny country that wishes to enter the Security Council should enter from the main gate. Back door diplomacy can never replace the requisite majority prescribed by the Charter'.[28]

Italy fell into line with NAM's position, as it feared that its opposition to elevating Germany and Japan to permanent member status could be overridden if a plan similar to that proposed by Razali were actually adopted. Fulci, the Italian Ambassador in the UN, claimed that since Razali realized that some aspirants to permanent seats could not command the votes of two-thirds of the UN members, he 'devised a procedural short-cut, a legal maneuver'.[29] He broke the reform down into phases in order to give some states the chance to become permanent members by gaining easily the support of a lower majority than that required in Article 108. Like the non-aligned states, Italy focused its criticism on Razali's proposition for an enlargement of the Council in three separate stages with different majorities and was very critical of the idea of passing the first two resolutions by a majority of two-thirds only of those *present and voting*. Italy invoked the General Assembly's usual methods of voting in an attempt to explain its opposition to the plan, namely that when the time comes for voting on thorny issues a significant number of states prefer either to abstain or to be absent out of fear of offending 'either the con-tender or the other by their decision'.[30] The voting records clearly show, Italy went on, that often no more than 120 states actually participate in a vote, reducing the required majority to 80, less than half of the General Assembly's membership. Italy complained that 'Razali and the pretenders to permanent seats devised this procedural artifice to force through a decision that would first institute new permanent seats and then designate the beneficiaries by a majority as low as less than half the entire UN membership'.[31] This would have the bandwagon effect of easing the passage of the third resolution by a majority of two-thirds of all member states as provided for by Article 108.[32] In a clear attempt to polarize the debate in the General Assembly, Fulci asked emphatically: 'can any great country really expect to enter the Security Council not by the main door of Article 108, but by the back door of Article 18 of the Charter?'.[33]

Wrangles over procedures

The immediate result of the polarization of the debate was the formation of the 'Coffee Club', an Italy-led coalition of developed and developing states opposed to the Razali plan. The Coffee Club 'represented a *de facto* alliance' of those, who through joint diplomatic initiatives, wanted to work against the Razali plan.[34] Its positions coincided with those of the NAM. Its role proved to be decisive in the ensuing debate on Council reform. Its initiatives sparked off an acrimonious discussion during the 1997 and 1998 sessions of the General Assembly and the Open-Ended

Working Group and, at the end of the day, led member states to turn down the Razali proposal. The question 'who is afraid of Article 108', routinely put by Italy and other members of the Coffee Club, most of which belonged to the NAM, distracted the two forums from the important issue of Security Council enlargement by shifting the discussion to the legal issue of the required voting threshold for Charter amendments. The subsequent discussions showed how the member states could employ legal technicalities to suppress pressing political realities.

Things came to a head when Italy tabled on 22 October 1997 a draft resolution on Council reform. The draft resolution A/52/L.7, which was co-sponsored by other members of the Coffee Club (Canada, Egypt, Guatemala, Lebanon, Mexico, Pakistan, Qatar, Syria and Turkey) proposed more time for negotiations and stressed that the matter of Council reform should not be subjected to any imposed time frame. According to the draft resolution, a rash approach bound to an unrealistic and rigid timetable was not appropriate, the situation simply not yet being ripe for a political decision on major issues of reform. But the most important part of the draft resolution was that which provided that 'any resolution with Charter amendment implications' must necessarily be adopted by a two-thirds majority of the UN membership, as stipulated in Article 108 of the UN Charter.[35]

Japan and Germany reacted promptly to the Italian initiative. The Permanent Representative of Japan to the UN sent a letter to all UN members the next day. He underlined that significant progress had been made in the discussions on Council reform and urged them not to support or co-sponsor the draft resolution. The chief diplomat of Japan wrote to the member states:

> it is feared that this draft, in practical terms, will kill the momentum generated this year and brings the movement for serious negotiations to a standstill ... This draft resolution is unbalanced, and can only do harm to the creative efforts and the spirit of cooperation shown by most of the member states. Japan is ready to stand together with any member state against all attempts that would obstruct our effort. From this viewpoint, I strongly request that you will not associate yourself with this draft resolution.[36]

Germany not only sent a similar letter to the member states but, on 1 December 1997, it proposed amendments to draft resolution A/52/L.7[37] which suggested the application of Article 18 of the UN Charter for General Assembly resolutions which were not direct Charter amendments. After hectic and difficult private consultations that were held among the member states at the initiative of the President of the General Assembly, the draft resolution of Italy and the amendment suggested by Germany were left on the table and not put to the vote. However, the vehement opposition of Germany and Japan to the Italian initiative reinforced to many of those who were against the Razali plan the suspicion that behind it one could detect the hand of Germany, Japan and the permanent members who wanted to promote the interests of the few. This, in turn, led more developing states to join the ranks of the Coffee Club which, as Fulci noted, from an initial 15 countries in 1997, increased to include more than 50 in 1998. The Club, according to the Italian Ambassador Paolo Fulci, who played a leading role in its formation, had the potential of mobilizing more than 130 states against the Razali plan.[38]

It was quite obvious that the Open-Ended Working Group, now in its fourth year of operation, had been converted into something that it ought not to be – a debating club unable to make any substantial contribution to the process of Council reform. A significant part of its work, after the first half of 1997, was diverted to the discussion of procedures for amending the UN Charter, about which the controversy showed no signs of mellowing. On the contrary, attitudes hardened in autumn 1998, with rumours rife that Germany, Japan and their main supporters (including Britain, France and the United States) were about to present to the General Assembly a new plan 'inspired by the two plus three rotational seats formula' and the voting procedures promoted by Razali. Once again, the Coffee Club members were mobilized and resolved that a new draft resolution on procedure be introduced in the Assembly on 28 October 1998. The draft resolution, named A/53/L.16, was co-sponsored by Italy, Canada, Spain and 24 developing states.[39] Draft Resolution A/53/L.16 provided more explicitly and emphatically than draft resolution A/52/L.7 of 1997 that 'any resolution with Charter amendment implications must be adopted by the two-third majority of the United Nations membership referred to in Article 108 of the Charter'. The language of draft resolution A/53/L.16 was a faithful reflection – word for word – of the Declaration regarding the reform of the Security Council issued by the heads of state or government of the members of NAM at their summit held in Durban from 29 August to 3 September 1998.[40] The sponsors of draft resolution A/53/L.16 clarified that the phrase 'any resolution with Charter amendment implications' referred to resolutions which contained proposals for concrete amendments to the UN Charter, or which could lead to the possible adoption of such amendments, or which provided criteria or elements for such amendments.[41]

Just as a law of physics says that every action is followed by a reaction, so the initiative of the Coffee Club members to table draft resolution A/53/L.16 provoked a response of a similar kind from an opposite alignment of states, led by Belgium. This group of states consisted of Western and Eastern European countries (among them, Austria, Belgium, Bulgaria, the Czech Republic, Denmark, Estonia, Hungary, Ireland, Luxembourg, Lithuania, the Netherlands, Portugal and Ukraine) plus India, Brazil and Uzbekistan, which appeared to be out of line with the rest of the non-aligned group and Australia. All these states had registered their support for the Razali plan, agreeing that the phased approach and the voting procedure prescribed in it were legally sound and politically legitimate. They admitted that the Charter could not be amended unless the provisions of Article 108 were adhered to, accepting the view that decisions on enlargement dealt with fundamental issues of UN structure and functioning. But, as they said, this did not necessarily mean that the first two resolutions, which would have implications only for Charter amendment, could not be adopted by the Article 18 voting rule. They voiced the same opinion in the Open-Ended Working Group and in the General Assembly: implications of Charter amendments were not actual amendments and therefore did not involve Article 108.

Following this legalistic line of reasoning further, they argued that it may be difficult to define an 'implication', and it would be much more difficult to define a resolution with an implication requiring the application of Article 108. They complained that draft resolution A/53/L.16 had been based on legally questionable arguments and that, in effect, it entailed amending the Charter through a voting procedure that was not provided for in the Charter. As Belgium put it, 'we doubt the objectivity of an argument that attempts to distort an Article of the Charter [i.e. Article 108] basing itself on the subjective and ambiguous notion of Charter amendment implications'.[42]

The members of the Belgium-led group accused the sponsors of draft resolution A/53/L.16 of being obstructionists, provoking unnecessary legal and political controversies and trying to do irreparable harm to the process of Council reform. But they did not restrict themselves only to verbal accusations. On 18 November 1998, they presented draft resolution A/53/L.42 as an amendment to draft resolution A/53/L.16. In essence, draft resolution A/53/L.42 provided that Article 108 applies only to the adoption of actual amendments to the UN Charter and, therefore, does not apply to resolutions, which only have implications for Charter amendments.[43] Draft resolution A/53/L.42 was also sponsored by Britain, France, the United States, Germany and Japan, all of which denied allegations made by the members of the Coffee Club that they were about to table a new reform plan that would allow the 'two plus three' formula to be passed.[44] They proceeded, however, to underline that they had decided to sponsor draft resolution A/53/L.42 in order to keep all the negotiating options open.[45] The two other permanent members, Russia and China, chose to fall into line with the opposite side.[46]

Despite the efforts made to reconcile the views of the two sides, the sponsors of draft resolution A/53/L.16, the number of which in the meantime had risen from 25 to 34 states, stuck to their decision to put it to a vote.[47] They appeared resolved to clear up procedural uncertainties which had been hanging over the Security Council reform process and in this way to avert the permanent three (Britain, France and the United States) from taking sudden initiatives. The opposite alignment of states, realizing that its draft resolution would be outvoted by the majority of member states, gave in. They withdrew their draft resolution A/53/L.42 and opted for the alternative resolution. They did so in order to save face, Fulci explained. On 23 November 1998, after some alterations to its text, the draft resolution A/53/L.16 was unanimously adopted by the General Assembly as Resolution 53/30. In essence, the meaning of Resolution 53/30 was that there could be no distinction between procedural, framework or amendment resolutions and that the two-thirds majority rule was required to undertake any kind of Council reform in the future.[48]

In conclusion, Resolution 53/30 terminated any possibility of adopting reform proposals akin to the Razali plan. After many fruitless discussions and much discord in the discussions that took place in 1998 and 1999, a large number of states, mostly from the NAM, shifted their focus from demanding permanent seats on the Council to the less controversial issue of expanding non-permanent membership. They believed that the permanent five would be more likely to make progress on this issue. Having taken this position, all hopes for substantial comprehensive reform of the Security Council were dashed, dampening the optimism of Germany and Japan and certain other states for obtaining permanent seats.

The General Assembly, through the UN Millennium Declaration adopted on 8 September 2000, expressed the resolve of its membership to intensify efforts to achieve a comprehensive Council reform. To this effect, in the remaining months of 2000 and in 2001, the General Assembly and the Open-Ended Working Group on Council Reform dedicated a large number of sessions to debating a sound and acceptable settlement of the issues involved. During these sessions it became apparent once again that the membership of the UN was still unable to reach even a minimum common position. What was clearly manifested was the debate's polarization between, on the one hand, the permanent five which felt that the current structure of the Council suited them fairly well and were happy to delay substantial reform for as long as possible and, on the other hand, the rest of the UN membership which continued to demand in one way or another reform of the Council. It seemed that the efforts to overhaul the Security Council would drag on for years to come.

6 Conclusions

The Security Council was formed mainly by the victorious states of 1945 with a view to be the executive organ of the UN holding authority over the most important UN activities. The Security Council was built up around the realistic conviction that its structure, for reasons of effectiveness, should have integrated within it the element of power and should reflect on a small scale the membership of the UN. The element of power was embedded in the structure of the Security Council through the creation of a select group of five permanent members, which were given special privileges including the coveted right of veto over questions of substance which came before it. The idea that its composition should be more or less proportionally representative of the UN membership was materialized through the addition of six non-permanent members, thus raising the total size of the Council to 11 members.

The Security Council was established in accordance with the realities of 1945 but, as a dynamic and flexible institution of the UN, has had to keep its structure abreast of the changes in the world environment in which it has lived ever since. It follows that the reform of the Security Council is not an end in itself but rather an essential means of it retaining its relevance to an evolving world. The need arises for the institutional structure of the Security Council to be periodically overhauled in order to avoid facing the danger of remaining behind the reality in which it is supposed to function.

During the first ten years of the Security Council's operation there were relatively few complaints. Such demands started to be raised from 1955 and onward as many new independent states emerged in Asia and Africa in the course of the historical process of decolonization and became UN members. As a result, the general membership of the world organization was doubled during the period 1955–60. The dramatic increase in UN membership, which continued unabated until 1963, upset the ratio of the total number of members of the UN to the number of seats in the Security Council and brought about pressures for a reconsideration of the original composition of the Security Council and, more particularly, its non-permanent category. A large number of small and medium states called into question the original membership of the Security Council, casting doubts on the validity of the gentlemen's agreement of 1946, on the basis of which the non-permanent seats had so far been geographically distributed.

The debate on enlargement began with the Latin American states taking the initiative in 1956 and continued with the untiring support of African and Asian States. The latter became the most militant among the proponents of reform and were solidly in the forefront of demanding Security Council enlargement because their regions had not been given representation on the Security Council by the gentlemen's agreement of 1946. Having become the strongest numerical force in the UN, the Afro-Asian group of states claimed that they should be given seating in the Security Council proportionate to their membership in the UN. They turned down proposals for the replacement of the 1946 gentlemen's agreement by a new agreement that would reallocate the six non-permanent seats in the 11-member Security Council, taking into account the Afro-Asian claims for representation. Instead, they made strenuous efforts to entrench UN members in a debate about Security Council expansion.

In the period between 1956 and 1960 they leaned towards accepting proposals, such as those of the Latin American states, for an expansion of the Security Council from 11 to 13 by the addition of two non-permanent seats. However, the dramatic increase in the number of African and Asian members of the UN in the period 1960–3 made the group of Afro-Asian states, which by 1963 constituted more than half the UN's membership, more assertive and demanding. Accordingly, they tabled their own proposal, which called for an increase of the non-permanent seats from six to ten (and thereby an increase in the total membership of the Security Council from 11 to 15) and a change in the number of votes required for Security Council decisions from seven to nine. Their proposal also called for the replacement of the earlier gentlemen's agreement of 1946 and the election of the non-permanent members possibly on the basis of a newly agreed formula for regional distribution. According to this formula, the ten non-permanent seats would be allocated as follows: five would be drawn from African and Asian states, two from Latin America and Caribbean states, two from Western Europe and others and one from Eastern European states. Their proposal, which was tabled in the form of a draft resolution in the General Assembly, was approved by an overwhelming majority of the General Assembly in 1963. It constituted an amendment of Articles 23 and 27 of the UN Charter and came into effect in 1965, when two-thirds of all the members of the UN deposited their instruments of ratification according to the requirements of Article 108 of the UN Charter.

The eight-year long and sometimes acrimonious debate on Council expansion (1956–63) was successful for two reasons. One had to do with the attitude of the permanent five which did not make a determined stand

against the demands for enlargement of the Security Council's membership. From the start of the debate in 1956, the permanent five kept a low
profile on the Council's expansion and although they would have preferred
the maintenance of the status quo, they made clear that they would not
resist demands for reform of the Security Council which involved the least
possible changes to its structure. They were convinced that due to the large
rise in UN membership, imbalances in representation had become so
obvious that enlargement of the Security Council was inevitable. They
were of the view that the addition of four new non-permanent seats was
optimal from a political point of view. It would provide the Afro-Asian
states with more adequate representation, yet it would disturb as little as
possible the basic elements of the Council's structure. It would not alter
the number of permanent members, nor would it affect the privileged position of the permanent five, where the veto power exclusively reserved for
them would be left intact. That meant that the power of the permanent
five to exercise 'negative influence', that is their ability to prevent the
Council from taking decisions, would not be weakened. What would be
slightly impaired would be the power of the permanent five to exercise
'positive influence', that is their ability to get a Council resolution adopted.
Despite this, the permanent five appeared to consider an agreement for the
addition of four new non-permanent seats as the best alternative, the
alternative being a breakdown of the negotiations that could lead, sooner
or later, to an upsurge of pressures for enlarging the Council, not least its
permanent membership.

The debate on Council's expansion was also successful because the attitude of the Afro-Asian states was solid on this question and included the
support of all the Latin American states and also of the West Europeans,
with a few exceptions. The Afro-Asian states acted with unity to encounter
Soviet obstructionism, which, as seen in Chapter 2, was largely responsible
for the prolongation of the debate on Council expansion for years. While
the Soviet Union and its allies were in principle in favour of Council
expansion, they made such expansion conditional upon (i) the satisfaction
of their demand for tripartite control of the UN Secretariat and (ii) the
restoration of communist China's rights in the UN. As a result of the rigid
attitude of the Afro-Asian states, which constantly refused to recognize a
linkage of Council expansion with the aforementioned issues and especially with the Chinese issue, the Soviet Union softened its position and
finally acquiesced to Afro-Asian demands for unconditional support to
Council expansion.

The successful expansion of the composition of the Security Council
gave satisfaction to the majority of the member states and eliminated
almost all pressures for Council reform. As a matter of fact, the question
of Security Council reform was shelved for many years despite the fact that
the UN membership continued to grow constantly after 1965. From 1979
and during the 1980s, India along with a number of Afro-Asian states

belonging to NAM, tried to raise the issue of further expansion of the Security Council. However, due to the strong opposition of the permanent five and a large number of states from Europe to discuss any proposal relating to Security Council reform, the negotiations did not take off. The issue of Council reform hovered in the background in the 1980s only to return to the forefront in the early 1990s.

Indeed, the dynamic global changes that occurred from the mid-1980s to the early 1990s, and more particularly the collapse of communist rule in Eastern and Central Europe and the shift in the distribution of power, had a forceful impact on the UN and the Security Council. A manifestation of this impact was the increase in the UN membership, which rose from the original 51 in 1945 to 183 in 1992. Given the changes that had occurred, it was felt that the Security Council should adapt to the new international setting, one basic reason being that the increased membership of the UN had seriously affected the principle of representation, thus posing questions about the legitimacy of the decisions adopted by the Security Council. Due to these changes and the fact that the Security Council, owing to the radical shift in Soviet policy towards the UN, had begun from 1990 to play more than ever before an active role in world issues, the idea of reform of the Security Council gained momentum. Germany and Japan started publicly to voice their aspirations for permanent membership of the Council, Italy put forward its proposal for an EU common seat at the Council, while a large number of states – mostly from the less developed world – began to make complaints about the Council's unrepresentative character and the arrogant exercise of power by the permanent five.

All this generated pressures for discussing the issue of Security Council reform in the UN but the permanent five, which wanted to preserve the status quo in the Council, did their utmost to avert the UN from considering the issue. The Security Council was no longer a stage for East–West rivalry and the rediscovered unity and cooperation among the permanent five, especially shown during the Gulf crisis, made the idea of an active and productive post-Cold War Security Council seem viable. This gave ground to the permanent five to express reservations about the prospect of discussing the issue of Council reform in the UN. Their reservations were based on the argument that the Security Council, since the beginning of 1990, had started to fulfil effectively its primary responsibility for international peace and security, and therefore, there was no need for reform. In an attempt to contain a debate on Council reform, the permanent five acted in concert and in some haste to ensure that Russia, after the collapse and the formal dissolution of the Soviet Union in December 1991, would inherit the latter's permanent seat and privileges in the Security Council without debate in the UN. The permanent five felt anxious about what might happen if Russia was not considered automatically as the successor to the Soviet Union but was forced to go through the UN Charter procedure of applying as an aspiring member. If the Russian issue had to be discussed and decided upon in the General Assembly, it might prompt the whole UN membership to call into question the composition of the Security Council, thus raising demands for broader changes. As explained in Chapter 3, the high-profile meeting of the Security Council in January 1992, which conferred on Russia a *de facto* recognition as the successor to the permanent membership of the Soviet Union, was convened by Britain with the support of the other permanent members, all of which had good reasons to defer any re-examination of the Council's composition and membership rights.

The issue of Council reform under the item entitled 'Question of Equitable Representation on and Increase in the Membership of the Security Council' remained on the agenda of the General Assembly but its consideration was postponed throughout 1990–2. However, in 1993 a near-global consensus emerged on the need for a thorough review of the structure of the Security Council. Germany and Japan decided openly to pursue a permanent seat on the Council, while a large number of medium and small states, mostly from NAM, put strong pressure on the UN General Assembly to consider the issue. The permanent five were no longer able to contain discussion of the issue in the UN.

By the end of 1993 the question of reform was included in the deliberations of the General Assembly, which established a special subsidiary group to discuss and examine the question of Council reform and all relevant issues. When the 'Open-Ended Working Group on the Question of Equal Representation on and Increase in the Membership of the Security Council' started its proceedings in 1993, the three Western permanent members, changed their status quo position and gave lukewarm support to Japan's and Germany's candidatures. Washington, London and Paris made their support conditional on Bonn and Tokyo committing themselves not only to increasing their financial contribution to the UN budget but, more importantly, to being able and willing to take part in UN peacekeeping and peace-enforcement operations (the so-called military criterion). This meant (i) that the three Western permanent members were prepared to accept only a limited reform of the Security Council by the addition of two seats in the category of permanent membership, and (ii) that the obstacles to be surmounted for the satisfaction of the German and Japanese claims for permanent membership were still considerable. They had to do not only with the ability of the two candidates to take the necessary steps to meet the military criterion, but also with the thorny question of the extension of the veto power to new permanent members which, because the three permanent members had avoided taking a stand on it, remained unresolved. It is worth saying that the conditional acceptance of the Japanese and German candidates had not been overtly supported by Russia and China which had, in the meantime, professed themselves in favour of Council reform but had avoided openly supporting the candidacies of any country.

The conditional support expressed for Japan's and Germany's claims for permanent membership pushed the two candidates to work hard from 1993 onwards on improving their credentials for permanent seats: both states, which had started from the early 1990s to assume additional financial responsibilities, raised further their contributions to the UN budget as well as to its budget for peacekeeping operations. However, by 1995 neither country had fully met the military criterion. They had yet to resolve the question of whether or not they would commit their forces to major UN peacekeeping and enforcement operations. In fact, both countries had adopted constitutional and legal regulations that allowed them to participate in peacekeeping operations abroad, but were facing severe political hurdles in employing their forces in other more significant military operations.

Up until the end of 1994, negotiations over the reform issue centred around an attempt by the permanent members to come to terms with the scenario for a limited increase embracing Germany and Japan alone (the so called quick-fix formula). However, the prospect of the Council becoming more heavily tilted in favour of the industrialized world caused resentment among many countries which made known to the permanent five that they would never accept the enlargement of the Council by only these two states. From 1995, they put forward or supported proposals that changed the political context of the Council reform debate and shifted the focus away from the scenario of limited increase (the quick-fix formula) and towards making the Council more representative of the UN membership.

First, among them, were the states of NAM that sought an expansion of the total membership (permanent and non-permanent) of the Council of up to 26 seats. An overwhelming majority of NAM linked the accession of Germany and Japan to the Security Council's permanent membership with the simultaneous inclusion in the permanent membership of certain states from the less developed world. There were two main groups of states within the ranks of NAM, each group holding different positions as to a number of crucial issues. The first group, consisting of states mostly from Latin America and Asia, were in favour of the so-called 'two plus three' formula, whereby two permanent seats would be assigned to Germany and Japan and three permanent (named) seats to developing states (plus six non-permanent seats). Most of them, with a few exceptions such as India, were against the idea of extending the right of veto to the new permanent members. The second group, consisting mostly of African states belonging to NAM, sought the addition of more than three *rotating* permanent members from the less developed world in order to offset the imbalance that would be created by the inclusion of Japan and Germany into the club of permanent members and, at the same time, a corresponding increase in the non-permanent membership. They claimed that the veto power, as long as the permanent five continue to hold it, had to be granted to all new permanent members as well. There was also a smaller group of NAM states which opposed the idea of increasing the number of permanent seats and sought an enlargement only of the non-permanent category by 11 seats. Despite their divisions over the crucial issues of Council reform, all states of NAM promoted the view that the UN should aim at restricting the use of veto by the permanent members of the Council as a first step towards its abolition in the future.

Proposals put forward by the Nordic countries and other European states were quite different from the quick-fix formula supported by the permanent members. These countries sought to satisfy the different perspectives of NAM states by incorporating into their proposals elements from the proposals which, put forward by the main two groups of NAM, reflected the mainstream view. They proposed a Council which would number 23 or 25 members and would incorporate either the so-called 'two plus three' formula or the 'two plus three permanent rotating' formula whereby the three permanent seats allocated to developing states should be rotating. Most of them shared the view expressed by many NAM states that the new permanent members should be denied the right of veto.

Italy, which was against the above proposals, presented an alternative plan of its own. According to the Italian proposal, there would be no change in the number of permanent seats and the privileges of the permanent members would remain intact. However, in addition to the current ten non-permanent seats, a new class of ten *rotating* non-permanent seats would be created, thus increasing the total Council membership from 15 to 25. These new rotating seats would be occupied by states which, being selected on the basis of specified objective criteria and of a geographical distribution formula, would serve longer terms than the existing non-permanent members (i.e. more than two years). By the early days of 1996, a large number of states – among them Australia, Canada, Egypt, Spain and Turkey – had expressed support for or interest in the Italian formula.

It goes without saying that the adoption of any of these reform proposals would have impaired the status of the permanent five. First, an expansion of the permanent members with the addition of five or more new seats would shift the balance of power in the Security Council and would have a very negative impact on the special status of the permanent five states. Similarly, the increase of the total Council membership by the addition of 10 or 11 new state seats would mean that it would become more difficult for the permanent five to pass a substantive resolution. In other words, it would severely diminish what was termed in Chapter 1 as the 'positive influence' of the permanent five.

However, since the quick-fix formula had been dismissed as a non-realistic option, the permanent members felt compelled to modify their previous position and they began to discuss the need for a larger number of permanent members. From 1996 and onward, all except China came out in support of the 'two plus three' formula, whereby three out of five permanent seats would go to developing states. This represented the least damaging proposal from their standpoint since it envisaged an increase of the total membership of the Council to a maximum of 20 seats. Their position was that the Security Council should remain organized on the principle of responsibility and efficiency, rather than on the principle of representation. Their viewpoint was that the larger the Security Council, the less efficient its decision-making would be. They also communicated their intention to defend their own right of veto and opposed restrictions on the scope of the veto. They were probably more vehement on this burning issue than they were ever before.

The reform proposal of the permanent members had a double effect on the discussions: (i) it confounded further the candidacies of Germany and Japan and (ii) it made the reform process more perplexed than ever. Since four of the permanent members made Bonn's and Tokyo's accession conditional on the simultaneous elevation of three developing states to permanent membership, Germany and Japan had to forge a consensus with the developing states regarding their presentation in the club of permanent members. But this was a formidable task because Germany and Japan had already indicated a keen interest in enjoying equal veto rights with the existing permanent five, whereas at least half of the developing states (and a large number of European states) had been against the idea of granting the right of veto to any new permanent members. But apart from the contentious issue of veto, Germany and Japan had to wait for the developing states to agree among themselves as to which states would fill the three permanent slots and how they would do it. Discussions in the UN and elsewhere revealed the difficulties the developing states faced in reconciling their conflicting views. This was a highly complex task for the developing states because there were serious divisions among them over crucial issues related to the expansion of permanent members, such as the modalities and the criteria for the selection of new members. Finally, there had been striking differences between the developing states and the permanent members over the total size of the Security Council which had to be reconciled as well.

In 1997 Ismael Razali, the then General Assembly's President, made an attempt to reconcile the multiple differences between the member states. He put forward a three-stage reform plan that proposed the inclusion of five new permanent members (i.e. the 'two plus three' formula) and four new non-permanent members, thus bringing the total to 24 states. According to the Razali plan the five new permanent members would not get the veto power and would be selected by the General Assembly.

The Razali plan reflected the mainstream view and its implementation would have increased significantly UN membership representation, not least that of the developing states. However, this plan became, for reasons explained in Chapter 5, a matter of contention in the discussions that took place in 1997 and 1998 and it was finally rejected by the overwhelming majority of member states including Italy and members of NAM. They refused to discuss the merits of the plan with the permanent five. Italy turned down the Razali plan because its primary strategic concern, from the start of the debate on Council reform, was to counter any reform proposal which through a combination of increases in the permanent and non-permanent seats would result in granting Germany a permanent seat on the Security Council. The NAM called upon its members to kill the Razali plan because it considered that were the plan adopted, given the serious rift that still existed among NAM members on a number of crucial issues of reform, it would have caused great discord within its ranks and, as a consequence, serious repercussions for the unity of Movement. Thus, the NAM, for its own survival, tied its members down to an agreement not to go ahead with the Razali plan and, forming a common front with Italy, succeeded in mobilizing a very large number of states against the plan. As a result, it was removed from the negotiating table, thus bringing the debate on Council reform to an end in complete failure in the year 2000.

However, in one way or another member states continue to demand reform of the Security Council. It is an undisputed fact that the first and last time the Security Council underwent substantive reform was in 1965. But power realities have since changed dramatically, as some of the victorious powers of 1945 have lost their standing as great powers and new centres of power in the developed and developing world have emerged. However, despite this shift in global power and the great numerical expansion in UN membership since 1965, the Security Council has not undergone a second tranche of reform. The issue of reform, already paramount in the 1990s, has assumed historic proportions in the post-Cold War era. Whatever the outcome of the ongoing debate on the issue in question, one thing can be said with certainty: namely that a failure to reform the Security Council and bring it in line with contemporary realities will sooner or later lead to its deep alienation from the larger part of its membership and in turn to a greater crisis of legitimacy in the UN – a crisis it can hardly afford as it contemplates the next steps of its development in the twenty-first century. This is precisely what makes the current debate on Security Council reform such a crucial issue.

Appendix 1

The cascade effect of permanent membership

Position Paper by Argentina
UN Doc. A/AC.247/5 (a), 14 September 1995,
reprinted in UN Doc A/49/47 & A/49/965, 18 September 1995

1. The present working paper is only a first and preliminary attempt to examine, in both quantitative and comparative terms, the participation of the permanent members of the Security Council in the United Nations system as a whole.

2. When analyzed in contrast with United Nations institutional regulations, as stipulated in the Charter of the United Nations, a statistical study of the actual participation of the permanent members of the Security Council in the various organs of the system makes possible the identification of a problem intrinsic to the Organization's representative mechanism, namely, the large representation ratio of certain countries to the detriment of others.

3. Such a de facto situation is somehow analogous to granting a different status to a number of Member States in the system as a whole. Given its vast repercussions, it reflects a reality of the United Nations beyond the stipulations of the Charter.

4. We will, therefore, consider both the Charter and the representation figures separately, and take as a basis for comparison the situation of the five permanent members of the Security Council – France, China, the United States of America, the United Kingdom and the Russian Federation – to try to assess their overall representational advantage, as the centerpiece of the paper.

I. Regulations of the Charter of the United Nations

5. On the basis of Charter regulations, the status of permanent member has special bearing on:

   a) Voting prerogatives in the Security Council – veto right – (Art. 27)

   b) Composition of the Military Staff Committee (Art. 47), which consists of the Chiefs of Staff of the permanent members or their representatives;

c) Composition of the Trusteeship Council (Art. 86, b), integrated by the five permanent members. China joined the group in 1989.

6. As regards participation in the General Assembly, the Charter regulations postulate, inter alia, the following:

a) *General Committee*

(i) According to rule 31 of its rules of procedure, the General Assembly elects 21 vice-presidents. By decision 1 of the Assembly (in reference to resolution 33/138 of 19 December 1978), five of these vice-presidents are representatives of the five permanent members;

(ii) The General Committee is highly significant, given its role in assessing the provisional agenda and supplementary list of items, and introducing recommendations as to their inclusion in agenda rule 40;

(iii) On the other hand, permanent members may not assume the chairmanship of the General Assembly, or the chairmanships of the Main Committees. The latter conforms to rule 31, which indirectly indicates that the presidencies of the Assembly and chairmanships of the Main Committees cannot correspond to the same countries;

(iv) Likewise, it is established practice that the permanent members do not assume the posts of vice-chairman or rapporteur of the Main Committees;.

b) *Committee on Contributions*

Established by General Assembly resolution 14 (I) of 1946, this Committee advises the Assembly on matters relating to the allocation of the organization's expenses and on the application of Article 19 of the Charter in cases of arrears in the payment of contributions. Its membership has been expanded several times, now standing at 18. Members are selected by the General Assembly on the basis of geographical distribution, personal qualifications and experience. They serve for a period of three years, retire by rotation and are eligible for re-appointment.

II. Statistical findings

A. General Assembly

1. Committee on Contributions

7. For the period 1984–1993, an average of four permanent members belonged to the Committee in any given year, showing a 70 per cent re-appointment rate; that is, they succeeded in getting re-appointed – on average – 7 out of the 10 times they were eligible for re-appointment. On the other hand, non-permanent members have a 48 per cent re-appointment rate, that is, they succeeded in getting re-appointed a little under 5 out of 10 times when they were eligible for re-appointment.

2. Advisory Committee on Administrative and Budgetary Questions

8. Established at the first session of the General Assembly, by resolution 14 (I) of 13 February 1946, this particular Committee examines and reports on regular and peace-keeping budgets and accounts of the Organization,

as well as on the administrative budgets of the specialized agencies. It also advises the Assembly on other administrative and financial matters referred to it. Its membership has been expanded numerous times, now standing at a total of 16. Members are appointed by the Assembly on the basis of geographical distribution, personal qualifications and experience. They serve for three-year periods and retire by rotation, but are eligible for re-appointment.

9. For the period 1984–1993, an average of four permanent members served on the Committee in any given year. They presented a combined re-appointment rate of 70 per cent, with France, the United States of America and the Union of Soviet Socialist Republics/Russian Federation each presenting a 100 per cent re-appointment rate. On the other hand, non-permanent members have a combined re-appointment rate of 41 per cent, re-entering the Committee only 4 out of 10 times when they are eligible to do so.

   3. General Assembly ad hoc and subsidiary organs

10. Permanent members also take part in a number of important United Nations bodies dependent on the General Assembly:

   (a) *Committee on Applications for Review of Administrative Tribunal Judgements.*

   By its resolution 957 (X) of 8 November 1955, the General Assembly established a committee, authorized by paragraph 2 of Article 96 of the Charter, to request consultative opinions from the International Court of Justice on decisions of the Administrative Tribunal. The Committee is constituted by the members of the current or most recent General Committee, which includes permanent members;

   (b) *International Law Commission.*

   Established by resolution 174 (II) of 21 November 1947, the Commission was established by the Assembly with the function of encouraging the progressive development of International Law and its codification. Its membership has been expanded a number of times, now standing at a total of 34, and is elected on the basis of geographical distribution. With the sole exception of the United Kingdom, who did not participate for four years, the permanent members belonged to it continuously during the period 1984–1993. Other members rotated or were retired, at a rate of 20 per cent;

   (c) *United Nations Conciliation Committee for Palestine.*

   Established by resolution 104 (III) of 11 December 1948, this Committee was, inter alia, established by the General Assembly to help with the repatriation of refugees and to assist Israel and the Arab States to achieve final settlements on all questions outstanding between them. The Committee's regular members are France, Turkey, and the United States of America – two of them Security Council permanent members;

   (d) *United Nations Administrative Tribunal.*

   Established by the General Assembly by its resolution 351 A (IV) of 24 November 1949, the Tribunal hears and passes judgement on applications alleging non-observance of contracts of employment on the part of the United Nations Secretariat staff members or of their terms of appointment. Members are appointed by the Assembly on the recommendation of the Fifth Committee for a three-year term. For the period 1984–1993, at least three of the seven positions of the Tribunal corresponded, at any one time, to permanent members, with their tenure averaging 45 per cent of the total;

(e) United Nations Scientific Committee on the Effects of Atomic Radiation.

Established by the General Assembly by its resolution 913 (X) of 3 December 1955, the Committee reports on all major sources of exposure to ionizing radiation in the human environment and submits annual progress reports to the Assembly. Its membership has been expanded a number of times, now standing at a total of 21. With the exception of three years, in which only four of the five permanent members participated, the five permanent members were included continuously in the Committee during 1984–1993;

(f) Committee on the Peaceful Uses of Outer Space.

This Committee, established in 1959, acquired permanent status through General Assembly resolution 1721 (XVI) of 20 December 1961. Its membership has been gradually expanded to a present total of 53 members, which includes the five permanent members, on a continual basis;

(g) Special Committee on Peace-keeping Operations.

Established by the General Assembly by its resolution 2006 (XIX) of 18 February 1965, it consists of 34 members, including the five permanent members on a continual basis;

(h) Joint Inspection Unit.

Established by the General Assembly by its resolution 2150 (XXI) of 4 November 1966 and beginning its work in 1968, the Unit ensures that the activities undertaken by organizations of the United Nations system are carried out as economically as possible, with optimum use being made of available resources. It consists of no more than 11 Inspectors elected on the basis of equitable geographic distribution and serving in their personal capacity for a term of five years, which can be renewed only once. With the exception of China, permanent members averaged 3 Inspectors out of 11 at any one time;

(i) United Nations Commission on International Trade Law.

Established by the General Assembly by its resolution 2205 (XXI) of 17 December 1966, the Commission seeks to promote the progressive harmonization and unification of the law of international trade. Its membership has been expanded on several occasions, with a present total of 36 elected on the basis of six-year terms. With the exception of 1985, when only four of the five permanent members participated, all five served continuously during the period 1984–1993. Other members rotated or were retired at a rate of 15 per cent;

(j) Committee on Relations with the Host Country.

Established by the General Assembly by resolution 2819 of 15 December 1971, it consists of 15 members nominated by the President of the Assembly, which includes the five permanent members on a continual basis;

(k) Consultative Committee on Disarmament.

Established in 1978 by the General Assembly by resolution S-10/2 of 30 June 1978, the Committee is composed of 20 eminent personalities, all nominated by the Secretary-General. It includes experts representing the five permanent members on a continual basis;

(l) Special Committee on the Charter of the United Nations and on the Strengthening of the Role of the Organization.

By its resolution 3499 of 15 December 1975, the General Assembly re-established the former Special Committee on the United Nations Charter under a new name. After a number of successive expansions, the Committee today consists of 47 members nominated by the President of the Assembly, including the five permanent members on a continual basis;

(m) Committee on Information.

Established by the General Assembly by its resolution 33/115 C of 18 December 1978, it has undergone successive expansions and currently consists of 83 members assigned by the President of the Assembly, including the five permanent members on a continual basis;

(n) United Nations Environment Programme.

Established in 1972 by General Assembly resolution 2997 (XXVII) of 15 December 1972, UNEP is represented by a Governing Council whose functions are, among others, to promote international cooperation in the environment field, recommend policies to this end and provide general policy guidance for the coordination of environmental programmes within the United Nations system. The Council reports to the Assembly through the Economic and Social Council and is composed of 58 members elected by the Assembly on the basis of geographic distribution and four-year terms. For the period 1984–1993, the five permanent members averaged 10 full years of participation, thus covering the entire period. The rest of the members combined – averaged eight years of participation;

(o) Human Rights Committee.

Based on available information for the period 1986–1993, three permanent members participated in this Committee continuously during the given period, while the rest of the membership was subject to rotation or changes at a rate of 12 per cent;

(p) Committee on the Elimination of Racial Discrimination.

Established by the General Assembly by its resolution 2106 (XX) of 21 December 1965, it consists of 18 experts elected by the Assembly on the basis of geographic distribution. For the period 1984–1993, two permanent members were added to two others (who had already been on the Committee) in 1986, after which all four served on a continual basis. On the other hand, other Committee members were rotated or retired at a rate of 21 per cent.

B. Economic and Social Council
11. The five permanent members are also part of the Economic and Social Council and various standing organs of limited membership, re-elected successively since the establishment of such organs.
1. Economic and Social Council (general membership)
12. Consisting originally of 18 members, it was successively expanded to include its present total of 53 members with three-year terms. Eighteen of these are nominated every year in General Assembly elections. With the exception of China, the five permanent members belonged to it almost continuously from its beginnings, until 1993 (combined default time: two years). Combined default time: total time of non-participation. For the period 1984–1993, they averaged 10 full years of participation (100 per cent), while all other members – combined – averaged 3.9 years of partici- pation (39 per cent) in the same period. Figure 1 (sample graph) [not shown here] of the appendix shows this result. Figure 2 [not shown here] establishes the same comparison, but shows a breakdown of the compo- nent of the column "others" corresponding to Figure 1 (on the basis of geographical distribution).
2. Subsidiary organs of the Economic and Social Council
13. Permanent members have also taken part in a number of other import- ant United Nations bodies dependent on the Economic and Social Council:
   (a) *Statistical Commission.*
   Established by Economic and Social Council resolution 8 (I) of 1946, the Commission assists the Council in promoting the development of national statistics, coordinating the statistical work of certain specialized agencies and advising United Nations organs on questions regarding statis- tical information. Its membership has been expanded a number of times to a present total of 24, elected on the basis of equitable geographic distribu- tion. With the exception of China, the permanent members served on the Commission almost continuously from its inception until 1993 (combined default time: 3 years). For the period 1984–1993, they averaged 10 full years of participation (100 per cent). All other members combined aver- aged 3.2 years of participation (32 per cent) in the same period;
   (b) *Population Commission.*
   Established by Economic and Social Council resolution 3 (III) of 1946, the Commission studies and advises the Council on demographic questions and related social and economic matters. Its membership has been expanded successively since 1946, now standing at a total of 27. Members are elected by the Council for four-year terms on the basis of equitable geographic distribution. With the exception of China, the permanent members sat on the Committee continuously from its inception

until 1993. For the period 1984–1993, they averaged 10 full years of participation (100 per cent), while the rest of the membership averaged 2.7 years of participation (27 per cent) in the same period;

(c) *Commission for Social Development.*

Originally known as the Social Commission, it was established by Economic and Social Council resolution 10 (II) of 1946 and renamed in 1966. It advises the Council on social policies of a general character. Its membership, elected directly by the Council for four-year terms on the basis of geographic distribution, has been expanded a number of times and now stands at 32. With the exception of China, the permanent members served on the Commission almost continuously from its inception until 1993 (combined default time: 11 years). For the period 1984–1993, they averaged 8.8 years of participation (88 per cent), while the rest of the membership averaged 2.9 years of participation (29 per cent) in the same period;

(d) *Commission on Human Rights.*

Established by Economic and Social Council resolution 5 (I) of 1946, the Commission reports on questions regarding the international bill of rights and other related declarations on civil liberties and various forms of discrimination. Its membership has been expanded numerous times, now standing at a total of 53. Members are elected for three-year terms on the basis of equitable geographic distribution. With the exception of China, the permanent members were members of the Commission almost continuously from its inception until 1993 (combined default time: three years). For the period 1984–1993, they averaged 10 full years of participation (100 per cent). All other members averaged 3.5 years of participation (35 per cent) in the same period;

(e) *Commission on Transnational Corporations.*

Established by Economic and Social Council resolution 1913 (LVII) of 1974, the Commission comprises 48 members elected directly by the Council for three-year terms on the basis of geographic distribution. With the exception of China, the permanent members served on the Commission continuously from its inception until 1993. For the period 1984–1993, they averaged 10 full years of participation (100 per cent). The remaining members averaged 4.8 years of participation (48 per cent) for the same period;

(f) *Committee for Programme and Coordination.*

Established by Economic and Social Council resolution 920 (XXXIV) of 1962, the Committee functions as the main subsidiary organ of the Council and the Assembly for purposes of planning, programming and coordination. Its membership has been expanded a number of times to its present total of 34. Members are elected by the Council for three-year terms on the basis of equitable geographic distribution. With the exception of China, the permanent members sat on the Committee continuously from its inception until 1993. For the period 1984–1993, they averaged

9.4 years of participation (94 per cent), while all others averaged 3.7 years of participation (37 per cent);

(g) *Commission on Narcotic Drugs.*

Established by Economic and Social Council resolution 9 (I) of 1946, the Commission comprises a total of 53 members elected by the Council for four-year terms at two-year intervals on the basis of geographic distribution. With the exception of China, the permanent members served on the Commission continuously from its inception until 1993. For the period 1984–1993, they averaged 9.6 years of participation (96 per cent), while the rest of the membership averaged 5.2 years (52 per cent);

(h) *Commission on Human Settlements (Habitat).*

Established by the General Assembly by its resolution 32/162 of 19 December 1977, the Commission comprises a total of 58 members elected for three to four-year terms on the basis of geographic distribution. With the exception of China, the permanent members sat on the Commission continuously from its inception until 1993. For the period 1984–1993, they averaged 8.4 years of participation (84 per cent), while the rest of the membership averaged 5.5 years (55 per cent);

(i) *Commission on the Status of Women.*

Established by Economic and Social Council resolution 11 (II) of 1946, the Commission comprises a total of 45 members elected on the basis of equitable geographic distribution. With the exception of China, the permanent members participated in the Commission almost continuously from its beginnings until 1993 (combined default time: eight years). For the period 1984–1993, they averaged 8.6 years of participation (86 per cent), while the remaining members averaged a total of 3.7 years (37 per cent).

14. Appendix Figure 3 (sample graph) [not shown here] shows average participation of permanent and non-permanent members in the Economic and Social Council subsidiary organs mentioned above. Figure 4 [not shown here] establishes the same comparison, but shows a breakdown of the component "others" corresponding to Figure 3 (on the basis of geographic distribution).

C. International Court of Justice

15. Although the Statute of the International Court of Justice does not directly specify it, the five permanent members of the Security Council are de facto permanent members of the Court.

D. Related United Nations programmes and specialized agencies

1. *International Atomic Energy Agency*

16. Beginning its activities in 1957, the Agency seeks to accelerate and enlarge the contribution of atomic energy to peace, health and prosperity throughout the world. Its executive organ is the Board of Governors, members of which are designated on an annual basis by the Board itself

and on a bi-annual basis by the Agency's General Conference, all by the principle of equitable geographic distribution. With the exception of China, the permanent members have sat on the Board continuously since 1957. For the period 1984–1993, all five averaged 10 years of participation (100 per cent); other members combined averaged 3.1 years of participation (31 per cent) in the same period.

2. *International Civil Aviation Organization*

17. Beginning its activities in 1947, ICAO fosters the planning and development of international air transport so as to ensure a safe growth of civil aviation throughout the world. Its executive body is the members' Council, composed of 33 contracting States. Permanent members participated in the Council for an average of 35.6 years (possible total: 46 years) between 1947 and 1993, that is, almost 80 per cent of the total time. For the period 1984–1993, all five averaged 10 full years of participation (100 per cent), while the rest of the membership averaged 1.8 years of participation (18 per cent) in the same period.

3. *Food and Agriculture Organization of the United Nations*

18. Established in 1945, FAO includes a main Council as its chief executive organ, composed of 49 member nations elected by the FAO Conference for three-year terms. With the exception of the Russian Federation, which is not a member, the permanent members averaged 10 full years of participation (100 per cent) in the period 1984–1993; the rest of the membership averaged 2.7 years of participation (27 per cent) in the same period.

4. *International Maritime Organization*

19. Established in 1959, IMO regulates standards of maritime safety and facilitates cooperation among Governments on technical matters affecting international shipping. Its chief executive body is the IMO Council, composed of 32 members. With the exception of China, the permanent members have sat on the Council continuously since 1959. For the period 1984–1993, all five averaged 10 full years of participation (100 per cent), while the rest of the membership averaged 1.8 years (18 per cent) in the same period.

5. *International Telecommunication Union*

20. The Union's chief executive organ is its Council, the members of which are elected by the ITU Conference and are eligible for re-election (total Union membership is 183). With the exception of the United Kingdom, the permanent members have been members of the Council continuously since 1947. For the period 1984–1993, all five averaged 9.2 years (92 per cent) of participation in the Council, while the rest of the membership averaged 1.9 years (19 per cent) in the same period.

6. *World Meteorological Organization*

21. WMO became a specialized agency in 1951, with the WMO Executive Council serving as its chief executive body. Permanent members sat on the Council for an average of 31 years (possible total: 42 years) between 1951 and 1993, that is, 75 per cent of the total time. For the period 1984–1993,

all five permanent members averaged 8.7 years (87 per cent) of participation, while the rest of the membership averaged 1.8 years (18 per cent) in the same period.

7. *World Health Organization*

22. WHO became a specialized agency in 1948, with the WHO Executive Board serving as its chief executive organ. Permanent members served on the Board for an average of 36 years (possible total: 45 years) between 1948 and 1993, that is, 80 per cent of the total time. For the period 1984–1993, all five permanent members averaged 9.2 years (92 per cent) of participation, while the rest of the membership averaged 2 years (20 per cent) of participation in the same period.

8. *United Nations Educational, Scientific and Cultural Organization*

23. The organization was established in 1945. Its chief executive organ, the Executive Board, is elected by the UNESCO General Conference and consists of 51 member States who appoint representatives for four-year terms on the basis of geographic distribution. For the period 1984–1993, China, the Russian Federation and France were members of the Board continuously (10 full years of participation), while the rest of the membership averaged 3 years (30 per cent) of participation in the same period.

9. *United Nations Children's Fund*

24. Originally established as the United Nations International Children's Emergency Fund in 1946, it became a full permanent organ by General Assembly resolution 802 (VII) of 15 September 1953. Its leading executive body is the Executive Board, comprising 36 members elected for three-year terms on the basis of geographic distribution. With the exception of China, the permanent members served on the Board continuously until 1993. For the period 1984–1993, they averaged 10 full years of participation (100 per cent), while the remaining members averaged 3.6 years (36 per cent) of participation in the same period.

10. *United Nations Development Programme*

25. Established by the General Assembly by its resolution 2029 (XX) of 22 November 1965, UNDP includes a Governing Council as its chief executive organ. The Council's membership has been successively expanded – now standing at a total of 48 – and is elected on the basis of equitable distribution among "developed"' and "developing" countries as two separate categories. With the exception of China, the permanent members participated in the Board continuously until 1993. For the period 1984–1993, they averaged 10 full years of participation (100 per cent), while average participation for the remaining "developed" countries (excluding the United States of America, France, the United Kingdom and the Russian Federation) averaged 6.5 years (65 per cent).

11. *Office of the United Nations High Commissioner for Refugees*

26. Established by the General Assembly by its resolution 319 (IV) of 3 December 1949, UNHCR includes an Executive Committee as its leading

organ. The Committee's membership has been expanded a number of times, now standing at a total of 46 regular members, which includes (and has always included) all Security Council permanent members except for the Russian Federation.

12. *Universal Postal Union*

27. UPU became a United Nations specialized agency in 1948, with an Executive Council as its leading organ. For the period 1984–1993, the five permanent members averaged 6 years (60 per cent) of participation in the Council, while the rest of the membership averaged 2.1 years (21 per cent).

28. The above data make it somehow clear that the effective rates of participation of the five Security Council permanent members seem to be not directly reflective of Charter stipulations. In effect, they may be producing a certain degree of disequilibrium in the United Nations structure.

29. Such an apparent disequilibrium may find its roots in a number of reasons, which cause what can be called the 'cascade effect'. The permanent members' relative weight and negotiational advantage when soliciting their admittance into organs outside of the Security Council may well be reverberating throughout the Organization. The ongoing review of the Security Council may well grant all members an opportunity to look also in depth into this particular matter.

Appendix 2

Member states of the United Nations

Year	Original members
1945	Argentina, Australia, Belgium, Bolivia, Brazil, Belarus, Canada, Chile, China, Colombia, Costa Rica, Cuba, Czechoslovakia, Denmark, Dominican Republic, Ecuador, Egypt, El Salvador, Ethiopia, France, Greece, Guatemala, Haiti, Honduras, India, Iran, Iraq, Lebanon, Liberia, Luxembourg, Mexico, Netherlands, New Zealand, Nicaragua, Norway, Panama, Paraguay, Peru, Philippines, Poland, Russian Federation, Saudi Arabia, South Africa, Syrian Arab Republic, Turkey, Ukraine, United Kingdom of Great Britain and Northern Ireland, United States of America, Uruguay, Venezuela, Yugoslavia*a*

Year of admission	States admitted to the UN
1946	Afghanistan, Iceland, Sweden, Thailand
1947	Pakistan, Yemen
1948	Myanmar
1949	Israel
1950	Indonesia
1955	Albania, Austria, Bulgaria, Cambodia, Finland, Hungary, Ireland, Italy, Jordan, Lao People's Democratic Republic, Libyan Arab Jamahiriya, Nepal, Portugal, Romania, Spain, Sri Lanka
1956	Japan, Morocco, Sudan, Tunisia
1957	Ghana, Malaysia
1958	Guinea*b*
1960	Benin, Burkina Faso, Cameroon, Central African Republic, Chad, Congo, Côte d'Ivoire, Cyprus, Democratic Republic of the Congo, Gabon, Madagascar, Mali, Niger, Nigeria, Senegal, Somalia, Togo
1961	Mauritania, Mongolia, Sierra Leone, United Republic of Tanzania
1962	Algeria, Burundi, Jamaica, Rwanda, Trinidad and Tobago, Uganda

continued

Year of admission	States admitted to the UN
1963	Kenya, Kuwait
1964	Malawi, Malta, Zambia
1965	Gambia, Maldives, Singapore
1966	Barbados, Botswana, Guyana, Lesotho
1967	Democratic Yemen
1968	Equatorial Guinea, Mauritius, Swaziland
1970	Fiji
1971	Bahrain, Bhutan, Oman, Qatar, United Arab Emirates
1973	Bahamas, Federal Republic of Germany, German Democratic Republic
1974	Bangladesh, Grenada, Guinea-Bissau
1975	Cape Verde, Comoros, Mozambique, Papua New Guinea, Sao Tome and Principe, Suriname
1976	Angola, Samoa, Seychelles
1977	Djibouti, Viet Nam
1978	Dominica, Solomon Islands
1979	Saint Lucia
1980	Saint Vincent and the Grenadines, Zimbabwe
1981	Antigua and Barbuda, Belize, Vanuatu
1983	Saint Kitts and Nevis
1984	Brunei Darussalam
1990[c]	Liechtenstein, Namibia
1991	Democratic People's Republic of Korea, Estonia, Federated States of Micronesia, Latvia, Lithuania, Marshall Islands, Republic of Korea
1992	Armenia, Azerbaijan, Bosnia and Herzegovina[a], Croatia[a], Georgia, Kazakhstan, Kyrgyzstan, Moldova, San Marino, Slovenia[a], Tajikistan, Turkmenistan, Uzbekistan
1993	Andorra, Czech Republic, Eritrea, Monaco, Slovak Republic, The former Yugoslav Republic of Macedonia[a]
1994	Palau
1999	Kiribati, Nauru, Tonga
2000	Tuvalu, Serbia and Montenegro[a]
2002	Switzerland, Timor-Leste

Source: http://www.un.org/Overview/growth.htm (accessed 2 March 2004) (with permission from the UN).

Notes
a The Socialist Federal Republic of Yugoslavia was an original Member of the United Nations, the Charter having been signed on its behalf on 26 June 1945 and ratified 19 October 1945, until its dissolution following the establishment and subsequent admission as new members of Bosnia and Herzegovina, the Republic of Croatia, the Republic of Slovenia, The former Yugoslav Republic of Macedonia, and the Federal Republic of Yugoslavia.
    The Republic of Bosnia and Herzegovina was admitted as a Member of the United Nations by General Assembly Resolution A/RES/46/237 of 22 May 1992.
    The Republic of Croatia was admitted as a Member of the United Nations by General Assembly Resolution A/RES/46/238 of 22 May 1992.
    The Republic of Slovenia was admitted as a Member of the United Nations by General Assembly Resolution A/RES/46/236 of 22 May 1992.
    By Resolution A/RES/47/225 of 8 April 1993, the General Assembly decided to admit as a Member of the United Nations the State being provisionally referred to for all purposes

within the United Nations as 'The Former Yugoslav Republic of Macedonia' pending settlement of the difference that had arisen over its name.

The Federal Republic of Yugoslavia was admitted as a Member of the United Nations by General Assembly Resolution A/RES/55/12 of 1 November 2000.

Following the adoption and the promulgation of the Constitutional Charter of Serbia and Montenegro by the Assembly of the Federal Republic of Yugoslavia on 4 February 2003, the name of the State of the Federal Republic of Yugoslavia was changed to Serbia and Montenegro.

b The total remains the same because from 21 January 1958 Syria and Egypt continued as a single member (United Arab Republic).

c The Federal Republic of Germany and the German Democratic Republic were admitted to membership in the United Nations on 18 September 1973. Through the accession of the German Democratic Republic to the Federal Republic of Germany, effective from 3 October 1990, the two German States have united to form one sovereign State.

Appendix 3

Razali reform paper

Paper by the Chairman
of the
Open-Ended Working Group on the Question of Equitable Representation
on and Increase in the Membership of the Security Council and Other
Matters Related to the Security Council
20 March 1997

[Note that the paper takes the form of a draft resolution of the General Assembly]

The General Assembly

Recalling its resolution 48/26 of 3 December 1993,

Recognizing the primary responsibility of the Security Council for the maintenance of international peace and security under the Charter of the United Nations,

Recognizing also the functions and powers of the General Assembly on matters pertaining to the maintenance of international peace and security as contained in the Charter,

Welcoming closer cooperation between the Security Council and the General Assembly,

Noting that the effectiveness, credibility and legitimacy of the work of the Security Council depend on its representative character, on its ability to discharge its primary responsibility and in carrying out its duties on behalf of all members,

Reasserting the purposes and principles of the Charter and recalling that under Article 2(5) of the Charter, every Member State has pledged to 'give the United Nations every assistance in any action it takes in 'accordance with the present Charter'.

Stressing that the permanent members of the Security Council bear a special responsibility both to uphold the principles of the United Nations'

Charter and to give their full support to the Organisation's actions to maintain international peace and unity,

Acknowledging that there are many ways for Member States to contribute to the maintenance of international peace and security, and underlining that members of the Security Council should be elected with due regard to their record of various contributions to this end, and also to equitable geographical distribution, as noted in Article 23(1) of the Charter, and for their demonstrated commitment to and observance of international norms,

Recognizing the ongoing Report of the Security Council to improve its working methods,

Noting with appreciation the efforts of the Open-ended Working Group on the Question of Equitable Representation on and increase in the Membership of the Security Council and Other Matters Related to the Security Council, which began its work in January 1994,

Seeking Article 15 (1) of the Charter and Recognizing the need for enhanced cooperation between the Security Council and the General Assembly.

1. *Decides*:

a) to increase the membership of the Security Council from fifteen to twenty-four by adding five permanent and four non-permanent members;

b) that the five new permanent members of the Security Council shall be elected according to the following pattern:

(i)   One from the developing States of Africa;
(ii) One from the developing States of Asia;
(iii) One from the developing States of Latin America and the Caribbean;
(iv) Two from industrialised States;

c) that the four new non-permanent members of the Security Council shall be elected according to the following pattern:

(i)   One from African States;
(ii) One from Asian States;
(iii) One from Eastern European States;
(iv) One from Latin American and Caribbean States

2. *Invites* interested States to inform the members of the General Assembly that they are prepared to assume the functions and responsibilities of permanent members of the Security Council;

3. *Decides* to proceed by a vote of two-thirds of the members of the General Assembly by 28 February 1998, to the designation of the States that will be elected to exercise the functions and responsibilities of

permanent members of the Security Council, according to the pattern described in paragraph 1b, it being understood that if the number of States having obtained the required majority fall short of the number of seats allocated for permanent membership, new rounds of balloting will be conducted for the remaining category(ies), until five States obtain the required majority to occupy the five seats;

4. Recognizing that an overwhelming number of Member States consider the use of veto in the Security Council anachronistic and undemocratic, and have called for its elimination, *decides*

a) to discourage use of veto, by urging the original permanent members of the Security Council to limit the exercise of their veto power to actions taken under Chapter VII of the Charter;

b) that the new permanent members of the Security Council shall have no provision of the veto power;

5. *Decides* that for peacekeeping assessments, all new and original permanent members of the Security Council shall pay the same percentage rate of premium surcharge over and above their regular budget rate of assessment;

6. *Decides* that

a) no later than one week after the designation of States elected to serve as new permanent members of the Security Council, a resolution adopting amendments to the Charter arising from decisions taken in paragraphs 1, 3, and 4b will be put to the vote in accordance with Article 108 of the Charter of the United Nations

b) the resolution will also include amendments to Article 27(2) and (3) of the Charter to require the affirmative vote of 15 of 24 members of the Security Council for a decision;

c) the resolution will also include amendments to Article 53 of the Charter to delete reference to former enemies of its signatories, and to eliminate Article 107;

7. *Agrees* that the aforementioned amendments to the Charter in paragraph 6 a, b, and c shall come into force following ratification by State Members consistent with Article 108 of the Charter;

8. *Decides* that a review conference will be convened under Article 109 of the Charter of the United Nations, in ten years after the entry into force of the amendments described in the present resolution, in order to review the situation created by the entry into force of these amendments.

9. *Urges* the Security Council to undertake the following measures to enhance transparency and to strengthen the support and understanding of its decisions by the whole membership of the Organisation:

a) Implement fully and effectively its presidential statement of 16 December 1994, calling for greater recourse to open meetings of the Council, in particular at an early stage in its consideration of a subject;

b) Institutionalize regular monthly consultations between the President of the General Assembly and the President of the Security Council, together with the Chairs of the Main Committees of the General Assembly and members of the Security Council;

c) Conduct consultations between the President of the Security Council and the respective Chairs of the regional groups when necessary;

d) Conduct regular and substantive briefings by the President of the Security Council on informal consultations of the Security Council for all Member States;

e) Encourage consultations between members of the Security Council and the countries most affected by a decision of the Council;

f) Invite non-members of the Security Council to participate in the informal consultations of the Security Council under Article 31 and Article 32 of the Charter;

g) Institute provisions for the prompt convening of formal meetings of the Security Council no later than 48 hours after the request of a Member State of the United Nations;

h) Institutionalize a system of consultations during the decision-making process on the establishment, conduct, and termination of peace-keeping operations in order to strengthen the measures outlined in the presidential statement of the Security Council dated 28 March 1996;

i) Institutionalize the practice of giving opportunity to concerned states and organisations to present their views during closed meetings of the Sanctions Committees on issues arising from implementation of sanctions regimes imposed by the Security Council;

j) Implement fully and effectively the provisions on sanctions and Sanctions Committees as recommended by the Subgroup on the Question of United Nations Imposed Sanctions of the Informal Open-ended Working Group of the General Assembly on an Agenda for Peace;

k) Make available records of the Sanctions Committees to all Member States;

l) Operationalize Article 50 of the Charter, on the right of Member States to consult the Council with regard to a solution of their problems arising from implementation of preventive or enforcement measures imposed by the Council;

m) Hold frequent orientation debates before the Council takes a decision on a particular matter;

n) Encourage greater use of the 'Arria formula' to facilitate consultations between members and non-members of the Council;

o) Clarify what constitutes a procedural matter as reflected in Article 27(2) of the Charter;

p) Invite the participation of all Member States in the deliberations of the applicable subsidiary organs of the Council established in pursuance of Article 29 of the Charter;

q) Make greater use of the International Court of Justice by seeking its advisory opinion consistent with Article 96 (1) of the Charter;

r) Consult with regional organisations, agencies and arrangements, at appropriate levels, on matters affecting the maintenance of international peace and security in accordance with Chapter VIII of the Charter;

10. *Urges* the Security Council to issue its annual and special reports to the General Assembly taking into account General Assembly resolution 51/193 of 17 December 1996.

Notes

Introduction

1 See, for instance, T. Weiss, 'The illusion of UN Security Council reform', *The Washington Quarterly*, 26 (4), 2003, pp. 147–61; see also D. Caron, 'The legitimacy of the collective authority of the Security Council', *American Journal of International Law*, 87 (4), 1993, pp. 552–88. A large part of this article is devoted to the issue of Security Council reform.

2 See, for instance, B. Russett (ed.), *The Once and Future Security Council*, London: Macmillan, 1997. This volume is one of the major scholarly contributions ever written about Security Council reform; see also, P. Wallensteen, 'Representing the world: A Security Council for the 21st century, in P. Diehl, *The Politics of Global Governance*, Boulder: Lynne Reinner, 1997, pp. 103–15; M. Bertrand, 'The historical development of efforts to reform the UN' and P. Wilenski, 'The structure of the UN in the post-Cold period', in A. Roberts and B. Kingsbury (eds), *United Nations, Divided World. The UN's Roles in International Relations*, 2nd edn, Oxford: Oxford University Press, 1993, pp. 420–67; W.A. Knight, 'The future of the UN Security Council: questions of legitimacy and representation in multilateral governance', in A. Cooper, J. English and R. Thakur (eds), *Enhancing Global Governance. Towards a New Diplomacy*, New York: United Nations University Press, 2002, pp. 19–37; B. Fassbender, 'Pressure for Security Council reform', in D. Malone (ed.), *The UN Security Council. From the Cold War to the 21st Century*, Boulder: Lynne Rienner, 2004, pp. 341–55; see also J. Dedring, 'The Security Council', in P. Taylor and A.J.R. Groom (eds), *The United Nations at the Millennium. The Principal Organs*, London: Continuum, 2000, pp. 61–99; P. Taylor, S. Daws and U. Adamczick-Gerteis (eds), *Documents on Reform of the United Nations*, Aldershot: Darmouth, 1997, pp. 415–68.

3 See, for instance, R. Hiscocks, *The Security Council. A Study in Adolescence*, London: Longman, 1973, pp. 82–112; S. Bailey, *The Procedure of the UN Security Council*, 2nd edn, Oxford: Oxford University Press, 1988, pp. 107–45. There are only two single-authored books that have been written about the Security Council reform. The book written by B. Fassbender (*UN Security Council Reform and the Right of Veto. A Constitutional Perspective*, The Hague: Kluwer, 1998) follows a legalistic approach to the issue. R. Drifte's book (*Japan's Quest for a Permanent Security Council Seat*, London: Macmillan, 2000) analyses how Japan's bid for a permanent Security Council membership has been debated so far at the national and international level.

4 See, for instance, Commission on Global Governance, *Our Global Neighborhood*, Oxford: Oxford University Press, 1995, pp. 227–41; B. Urquhart and E. Childers, *Towards a More Effective United Nations*, Uppsala: Dag Hammarrskjold Foundation, 1992.

5 E. Luck, *Reforming the United Nations: Lessons from a History in Progress*, International Relations Studies and the United Nations Occasional Papers 2003, no 1, Academic Council on the United Nations, p. 4.

1 The Security Council in 1945 and the quest for reform

1 H. Briggs, 'Power politics and international organization', *American Journal of International Law*, 39 (4), 1945, p. 670.

2 The position of the permanent five in the Security Council had been somewhat analogous to that prescribed by political theorists as ruling elite within some specific political system. That is a well-defined group of people 'who to some degree exercise power or influence over other actors in the system'; see R. Dahl, 'A critique of the ruling elite model', *American Political Science Review*, 52 (2), 1958, p. 463.

3 See B. Russett, B. O'Neil and J. Sutterlin, 'Breaking the restructuring logjam', in B. Russett (ed.), *The Once and Future Security Council*, London, Macmillan, 1997, p. 157.

4 D. Lee, 'The genesis of the veto', *International Organization*, 1(1), 1947, p. 34.

5 K. Holsti, 'The concept of power in the study of international relations', *Background*, 7(4), 1964, pp. 188–92.

6 See Russett, O' Neil and Sutterlin, op. cit., p. 158.

7 H. Morgenthau, *Politics Among Nations*, New York: Alfred Knopf, 1968, p. 448.

8 F. Hinsley, *Power and the Pursuit of Peace*, Cambridge: Cambridge University Press, 1963, p. 340.

9 For the 'cascade effect' of permanent membership see Paper Position of Argentina, UN Doc. A/AC.247/5 (a), 14 September 1995. The text of the paper appears in Appendix 1.

10 Even pure institutionalist, like Lisa Martin, have admitted that 'institutions do reflect the power relations prevailing at the time of their creation, and tend to reinforce those relations, presumably directing a large share of the benefits they provide toward the most powerful'. See L. Martin, 'An institutionalist view: international institutions and state strategies', in T. Paul and J. Hall (eds), *International Order and the Future of World Politics*, Cambridge: Cambridge University Press, 1999, p. 93.

11 J. Morris, United Nations Security Council reform: A Counsel for the 21st Century', *Security Dialogue*, Vol. 31(3), 2000, p. 266.

12 A. Parsons, 'Britain and the Security Council', in E. Fisher (ed.), *The United Kingdom – The United Nations*, London: Macmillan, 1990, p. 49.

13 Roundtable on Security Council Reform. Available online at: www.ncrb.unac. org/unreform/roundtables/SCreform.html (accessed 5 January 2004).

14 E. Luck, *Reforming the United Nations: Lessons from a History in Progress*, International Relations Studies and the United Nations Occasional Papers 2003, no 1, Academic Council on the United Nations, p. 5.

15 Roundtable on Security Council Reform, op. cit.

16 For the notions of representation, legitimacy and efficiency and the relationship between them see D. Caron, 'The legitimacy of the collective authority of the Security Council', *American Journal of International Law*, 87(4), 1993, pp. 552–88; B. Fassbender, *UN Security Council Reform and the Right of Veto. A Constitutional Perspective*, The Hague, Kluwer, 1998, pp. 296–318; W.A. Knight, 'The future of the UN Security Council: questions of legitimacy and representation in multilateral governance', in A. Cooper, J. English and R. Thakur (eds), *Enhancing Global Governance. Towards a New Diplomacy*, New York, United Nations University Press, 2002, pp. 19–37; I. Claude,

'Collective legitimization as a political function of the United Nations', *International Organization*, 20(3), 1966, pp. 367–79; B. Russett, 'Ten balances for weighing UN reform proposals', in Russett, *The Once and Future Security Council*, op. cit., pp. 18–21; I. Hurd, 'Legitimacy, power and the symbolic life of the UN Security Council', *Global Governance*, 8(1), 2002, pp. 35–51; P. Wallensteen, 'Representing the world: A Security Council for the 21st century, in P. Diehl (ed.), *The Politics of Global Governance*, Boulder: Lynne Reinner, 1997, pp. 103–15; Morris, op. cit., pp. 265–77.
17 E. Carr, *The Twenty Years' Crisis*, 2nd edn, London: Macmillan, 1946, p. 29.

2 Demands for reform in the Cold War era

1 See C. Stavropoulos, 'The practice of voluntary abstention by permanent members of the Security Council under Article 27, paragraph 3, of the Charter of the United Nations', *American Journal of International Law*, 61(3), 1967, pp. 737–41.
2 See the views of J. De Arechaga, member of the International Law Commission, cited in. Stavropoulos, ibid., p. 747.
3 Y. Liang, 'Abstention and absence of a permanent member in relation to the voting procedure in the Security Council', *American Journal of International Law*, 44 (4), 1950, p. 707; for an account of the Security Council decisions taken with one permanent member abstaining see Stavropoulos, op. cit., pp. 743–5.
4 See UN Doc. GAOR, A/8/PV.45, 5 October 1953, para. 19
5 S. Bailey, *The Procedure of the UN Security Council*, 2nd edn, Oxford: Oxford University Press, 1988, p. 113.
6 R. Hiscocks, *The Security Council. A Study in Adolescence*, London: Longman, 1973, pp. 97–8.
7 For a detailed account of the way the Eastern European non-permanent seat was filled during this period see the excellent work of S. Bailey and S. Daws, *The United Nations. A Concise Political Guide*, 3rd edn, London: Macmillan, 1995, pp 40–1; see also N. Padelford, 'Politics and change in the Security Council', *International Organization*, 14 (3), 1960, pp. 384–5.
8 See the speech of Mr Martin, Permanent Representative of Canada to the UN, in the Ad Hoc Political Committee of the General Assembly, cited in UN Doc. A/AC.80/PV.25, 1 December 1955, p. 23. For the early efforts to solve the problem of membership see L. Gross, 'Progress towards universality of membership in the United Nations', *American Journal of International Law*, 50 (4), 1956, pp. 791–6.
9 See Appendix 2.
10 For the change in the membership of the various groups (i.e. the group of the Commonwealth states, the group of the Central European States, the group of the Western European states and the group of states from Africa, Asia and Middle East) see Padelford, op. cit., pp. 382–6. For the growth of the African membership in the UN see D. Kay, 'The impact of African states on the United Nations', *International Organization*, 23 (1) 1969, pp. 20–47.
11 Argentina, Bolivia, Brazil, Chile, Colombia, Costa Rica, Cuba, Dominican Republic, Ecuador, El Salvador, Haiti, Honduras, Panama, Paraguay, Peru and Venezuela.
12 See UN Doc. A/3138, A/3139 and A/3140, 26 June 1956; see also UN Doc. A/3446 and A/L.217/Rev.1, 19 December 1956.
13 For the question of Chinese representation in the UN see M. McDougal and R. Goodman, 'Chinese participation in the United Nations: the legal imperatives', *American Journal of International Law*, 60 (4), 1966, pp. 671–727.

14 E. Schwelb, 'Charter review and Charter amendment-recent developments', *International and Comparative Law Quarterly*, 7 (2), 1958, p. 316.

15 Ibid.

16 For details about the problem of Chinese Representation the United Nations see H. Briggs, 'Chinese representation in the United Nations', *American Journal of International Law*, 6 (2), 1952, pp. 192–209.

17 See *Yearbook of the United Nations, 1957*, New York: UN Office of Public Information, 1958, p. 115; *Yearbook of the United Nations, 1958*, New York: UN Office of Public Information, 1959, pp. 106–8; *Yearbook of the United Nations, 1959*, New York: UN Office of Public Information, 1960, p. 8. See also UN Doc. A/14/PV.841, 20 November 1959, p. 591.

18 Cited in E. Schwelb, 'Amendments to articles 23, 27 and 61 of the Charter of the United Nations', *American Journal of International Law*, 59 (4), 1965, p. 838.

19 See Appendix 2.

20 See UN Doc. A/SPC/L.52 and Add. 1–3, 1960, found in UN Doc. Report of the Special Political Committee, UN General Assembly, 15th session, Official Records, Agenda item no 23 (A/4626), 1960; see also *Yearbook of the United Nations, 1960*, New York: UN Office of Public Information, 1961, p. 205; see also Schwelb, 'Amendments to articles 23, 27 and 61 of the Charter of the United Nations', op. cit., p. 837.

21 See UN Doc. A/SPC/SR. 218, 6 December 1960 and UN Doc. GAOR, A/15/PV.960, 20 December 1960.

22 *Yearbook of the United Nations, 1960*, New York: UN Office of Public Information, 1961, p. 204.

23 Schwelb, 'Amendments to articles 23, 27 and 61 of the Charter of the United Nations', op. cit., p. 837.

24 R. Jackson, *The Non-Aligned, the UN, and the Superpowers*, New York: Praeger Publishers, 1983, p. 4.

25 Ibid.

26 See P. Willetts, *The Non-Aligned Movement. The Origins of a Third World Alliance*, London: Frances Pinter, 1978, p. 240.

27 See Yugoslav Government, *The Conference of Heads of State or Government of Non-Aligned Countries*, Belgrade: 1961, p. 89.

28 For the text of the final Declaration of the first conference of heads of state or government of non-aligned countries see O. Jankowitsch and K. Sauvant (eds), *Third World Without Superpowers: The Collected Documents of Non-Aligned Countries*, New York: Oceana Publications, 1978, pp. 3–7.

29 Ibid.

30 See *Yearbook of the United Nations, 1963*, New York: UN Office of Public Information, 1964, p. 80.

31 Ibid.

32 Ibid., p. 84; see also Schwelb, 'Amendments to articles 23, 27 and 61 of the Charter of the United Nations', op. cit., p. 840.

33 Ibid., p. 82.

34 Ibid., p. 83.

35 During this conference, the African states adopted a resolution calling that Africa, as a geographical region, should have equitable representation in the principal organs of the UN. Ibid., p. 81.

36 Schwelb, 'Amendments to articles 23, 27 and 61 of the Charter of the United Nations', op. cit., p. 840.

37 UN Doc. GAOR, A/18/PV.1285, 17 December 1963, p. 8.

38 Ibid., p. 9.

39 See UN Doc. A/SPC/SR.428, 14 December 1963.

40 See UN Doc. GAOR, A/18/PV.1285, op. cit., p. 15.

41 UN Doc. GAOR, A/18/PV.1285, 17 December 1963, p. 9.
42 Ibid., p. 10.
43 Ibid., p. 11.
44 See *New York Times*, 18 September 1963, p. 107.
45 S. Daws, 'The origins and development of UN electoral groups', in R. Thakur (ed.), *What is Equitable Geographic Representation in the Twenty-First Century*, Tokyo: The United Nations University, 1999, p. 19.
46 See G. Goodwin, 'The Expanding United Nations: I – Voting Patterns', *International Affairs* (Royal Institute of International Affairs), 36 (2), 1960, p. 180.
47 J. Teja, 'Expansion of the Security Council and its consensus procedure', *Netherlands International Law Review*, 16 (4), 1969, pp. 353–4.
48 W.A. Knight, 'The future of the UN Security Council: questions of legitimacy and representation in multilateral governance', in A. Cooper, J. English and R. Thakur (eds), *Enhancing Global Governance. Towards a New Diplomacy?*, New York: United Nations University Press, 2002, p. 21.
49 Teja, op. cit., p. 354.
50 For the informal consultations of the whole see D. Nicol, *The United Nations Security Council. Towards Greater Effectiveness*, New York: United Nations Institute for Training and Research, 1982, pp. 74–82; see also G. Berridge, *Return to the UN. UN Diplomacy in Regional Conflicts*, London, Macmillan, 1991, pp 3–11 and J. Dedring, 'The Security Council', in P. Taylor and A.J.R. Groom (eds), *The United Nations at the Millenium: The Principal Organs*, London: Continuum, 2000, pp. 75–9. See also informal consultations. Available online at: http:/www.globalpolicy.org/security/informal (accessed 5 December 2003).
51 Bailey, op. cit., p. 139.
52 C. Crowe, 'Some observations on the operation of the Security Council including the use of the veto', in D. Nicol (ed.), *Paths to Peace: The UN Security Council and its Presidency*, New York: Pergamon, 1981, p. 96.
53 Berridge, op. cit., p. 5.
54 J. Dedring, 'The Security Council', in Taylor and Groom, op. cit., p. 75.
55 See the final document of the third conference of the heads of state or government of the non-aligned countries, declaration on peace, interdependence, cooperation and democratization of international Relations, cited in Jankowitsch and Sauvant, op. cit., pp. 82–4.
56 See the final document of the third conference of Ministers of Foreign Affairs of the non-aligned countries, statement on international security and disarmament, ibid., p. 461; see also the communiqué of the consultative meeting of foreign Affairs of non-aligned countries at the United Nations during the 26th session of the General Assembly, ibid., pp. 501–8.
57 See the final document of the fourth conference of the heads of state or government of the non-aligned countries, political declaration, ibid., p. 203.
58 See the final document of the fifth conference of the heads of state or government of the non-aligned countries, political declaration, ibid., pp. 785–6.
59 See the final document of the sixth conference of the heads of state or government of the non-aligned countries, political declaration, in UN Doc. A/34/542, 11 October 1979, pp. 74–7.
60 See the final document of the seventh conference of the heads of state or government of the non-aligned countries, political declaration, in UN Doc. A/38/132 S/15675, 8 April 1983, pp. 48–50.
61 See UN Doc. GAOR, A/34/PV.103, 14 December 1979, pp. 1906–10 and UN Doc. GAOR, A/43/PV.104, 14 December 1979, pp. 1933–45 and especially p. 1944; see also *Yearbook of the United Nations 1979*, New York: UN Department of Public Information, 1982, pp. 435–6.

62 See all the *Yearbooks of the United Nations* that were issued by the UN Department of Public Information during the period 1980–90.

3 The post-Cold War case for reform

1 See M.S. Gorbachev, *Perestroika I Novoe myshlenie dlia nashei strany i idlia vsego mira*, Moscow: Politizdat, 1988.
2 See M. Gorbachev, 'Realities and guarantees for a secured world', *Pravda and Izvestia*, 17 September 1987.
3 J. Haslam, 'The UN and the Soviet Union: new thinking?, *International Affairs*, 65 (4), 1989, p. 681.
4 E. Sevardnadze, 'Introduction to a survey of the foreign and diplomatic activities of the USSR: November 1989–December 1990', *Vestnik Ministerstva Inostrannykh*, 22 January 1991.
5 Ibid. See also E. Sevardnadze, 'Address to the 45th session of the United Nations General Assembly', *Pravda*, 25 September 1990.
6 P. Shearman, 'New political thinking reassessed', *Review of International Studies*, 19 (2), 1993, p. 157.
7 *Izvestya*, 13 August 1991.
8 A.C. Lynch, 'The Realism of Russia's foreign policy', *Europe-Asia Studies*, 53 (1), 2001, p. 7; H. Adomeit, 'Russia as a great power in world affairs: images and reality', *International Affairs*, 71 (1), 1995, p. 35; S. Garnett, 'Russia's illusory ambitions', *Foreign Affairs*, 76 (2), 1997, p. 61.
9 C. Blacker, 'Russia and the West', in M. Mandelbaum (ed.), *The New Russian Foreign Policy*, New York: Council on Foreign Relations, 1998, pp 172–3; J. Checkel, 'Russian foreign policy: back to the future?', *RFE/RL Research Report*, 1 (41), 1992, p. 18.
10 *Diplomaticheskii Vestnik*, 4–5, 29 February–15 March 1992.
11 Between 1986 and 1995 the Soviet Union/Russia used the veto twice. For the changing patterns in the use of the veto in the Security Council see *Subjects of UN Security Council Vetoes*. Available online at: www.globalpolicy.org/security/membership/veto/vetosubj.htm (accessed 20 October 2003).
12 P. Taylor, *International Organization in a Modern World. The Regional and the Global Process*, London: Pinter 1995, p. 212.
13 Ibid.
14 The Security Council passed 37 resolutions in 1990, 42 in 1991 and 74 in 1992. It should be noted that in 1987 the Security Council adopted only 13 resolutions, in 1988 and 1989 it passed 20 resolutions per year; for details see S. Morphet, 'The influence of states and groups of states on and in the Security Council and General Assembly, 1980–1994', *Review of International Studies*, 21 (4), 1995, pp. 458–61.
15 M. Pedrazzi, 'Italy's approach to UN Security Council reform', *International Spectator*, 35 (3), p. 55.
16 See O. Croci, '*Italian security policy in the 1990s*', paper presented at the 52nd annual conference of the UK Political Science Association, held at the University of Aberdeen, 5–7 April 2002.
17 *The Financial Times*, 7 September 1990.
18 See S. Morphet, 'The Security Council and the General Assembly: Their interrelationship, 1980–1992', p. 12, paper presented at the joint sessions of the European Consortium for Political Research (ECPR), held at the University of Leiden, April 1993.
19 Report of the Secretary-General: Question of Equitable Representation on and Increase in the Membership of the Security Council, UN Doc. A/48/264, 20 July 1993, p. 82.

20 For the French position see the speech of Roland Dumas, the French Foreign Minister in the National Assembly in February 1991. Extracts from this speech can be found in *The Financial Times*, 19 February 1991. For German reactions to France's stance on this issue see *Frankfurter Allgemeine Zeitung*, 21 February 1991.

21 See S. Morphet, 'The influence of states and groups of states on and in the Security Council and General Assembly, 1980–1994', *Review of International Studies*, 21(4) 1995, p. 451. For the text of the Accra Declaration of the Foreign Ministers of NAM see UN Doc. A/46/659 of 19 November 1991 and UN Doc. A/46/726 of 4 December 1991.

22 UN Doc. GAOR, A/46/PV.68, 23 December 1991 and A/RES/46/418 of 11 December 1991.

23 See W.F. Schlor, *German Security Policy*, Adelphi Paper 227, London: International Institute for Strategic Studies, 1993, p. 57 and R. Drift, *Japan's Quest for a Permanent Security Council Seat. A Matter of Pride or Justice?*, Houndmills: Macmillan, 2000, pp. 60–2 and 118–24.

24 Drift, op. cit., p. 119.

25 H.L. Phippard, 'Remaking the Security Council: the options', in P. Taylor, S. Daws and U. Adamczick-Certeis (eds), *Documents on Reform of the United Nations*, Aldershot: Darmouth, 1997, p. 427.

26 For the reaction of Britain and France to the Italian proposal and the debate on the idea for a EU common seat, see P. Tsakaloyannis and D. Bourantonis, 'The European Union's common foreign and security policy and the reform of the Security Council', *European Foreign Affairs Review*, 2 (2), 1997, pp. 197–209.

27 Article J5.4 of the Maastricht Treaty on European Union.

28 Debates of the European Parliament, no 3-425/160, 16 December 1992.

29 See A.L. Bennett, *International Organizations: Principles and Issues*, New Jersey: Prentice Hall, 5th edn, 1991, pp. 80–2. For the relevant debate, arguments and counter-arguments, as well as for the text of General Assembly Resolution 2758 of 25 October 1971, see F. Kirgis, *International Organization in Their Legal Setting*, Minnesota: West Publishing Company, 1977, pp. 123–44.

30 See UN Doc A/47/60-S/23329, 30 December 1991, Annex II.

31 R. Rich, 'Recognition of states: the collapse of Yugoslavia and the Soviet Union', *European Journal of International Law*, 4 (1), 1993, pp. 45–6.

32 For an exposition of the legal view that 'all the states that arose from the dismemberment [of the USSR] should have become UN members through the admission procedure, with the exception of Byelorussia and the Ukraine, which were already members', and that 'this procedure should have been followed in so far as none of the new states, not even Russia, could have claimed to be the successor of the Soviet Union in the permanent Security Council seat', see B. Conforti, *The Law and Practice of the United Nations*, The Hague: Kluwer Law International, 1997, p. 45.

33 See Decision by the Council of Heads of State of the Commonwealth of Independent States, in UN Doc. A/47/60-S/23329, op. cit., Annex V.

34 See B. Fassbender, *UN Security Council Reform and the Right of Veto*, The Hague: Kluwer Law International, 1998, p. 184; see also C. Willson, 'Changing the Charter: The United Nations for the twenty-first century', *American Journal of International Law*, 90 (1), 1996, p. 118.

35 Moreover, in a written response to the author, dated 27 April 1998, by the Department of History and Documents of the Russian Foreign Ministry, it is stated that 'the UN Secretary-General and all representatives of the five permanent members of the Security Council agreed that [the USSR succession by Russia] does not need any approval or even consideration in the UN'. See

also Y.Z. Blum, 'Russia takes over the Soviet Union's seat at the United Nations', *European Journal of International Law*, 3 (2), 1992, p. 356, and N. White, *Keeping the Peace: The United Nations and the Maintenance of International Peace and Security*, 2nd edn, Manchester: Manchester University Press, 1997, p. 24. For a comprehensive account of 'the demise of the Soviet Union' see relevant section in Rich, op. cit., pp. 44–7.

36 See G. Samuels, 'Mixed reaction at the UN: Russia slips into the Soviet seat', *The New Leader*, 10–24 February 1992, pp. 5–7.
37 Ibid., p. 5.
38 See T. Daley, 'Russia's continuation of the Soviet Union's Security Council membership and prospective Russian policies toward the United Nations', Santa Monica, RAND, 1992, pp. 4–8.
39 *The Independent*, 24 December 1991.
40 Official Records of the European Communities, no C102, 22 April 1992, p. 47; see also *The Independent*, 24 December 1991, p. 1.
41 'Address to the Nation on the Commonwealth of Independent States', by President George Bush, 25 December 1991.
42 For the proceedings and the debate that took place during the Security Council summit of 1992 see D. Bourantonis and G. Kostakos, 'Diplomacy at the United Nations: The dual agenda of the 1992 Security Council summit', *Diplomacy & Statecraft*, 11 (3), 2000, pp. 212–26.
43 The fact that the initiative to convene the summit came from the British was confirmed by the Russian Foreign Ministry, Department of History and Documents, via fax sent to the author (fax dated 27 April 1998). See also Bourantonis and Kostakos, op. cit., p. 222.
44 *The Independent*, 7 January 1992; the title of the article, which refers to the preparatory stages of the Security Council summit, is very telling: 'UK finds a way to hold on the mother of all seats'.
45 Daley, op. cit., p. 8.
46 See Samuels, op. cit., p. 6.
47 M. Scharf, ' Musical chairs: The dissolution of states and membership in the United Nations, *Cornell International Law Journal*, 28, 1995, pp. 47–8.
48 See UN Doc. S/PV.3046, 31 January 1992, p. 47.
49 Ibid., p. 48.
50 Ibid.
51 Ibid.
52 Ibid., pp. 104–5.
53 *The Independent*, 7 January 1992.
54 See E. Matanle, *The UN Security Council. Prospects for Reform*, Discussion Paper 62, London: The Royal Institute of International Affairs, 1995, pp. 26–7.
55 UN Doc. S/PV.3046, op. cit., pp. 2–7.
56 UN Doc.A/47/277-S/24111 of 17 June 1992.
57 UN Doc.A/50/60-S/1995/1 of 3 January 1995.
58 UN Doc. S/PV.3046, op. cit., p. 141.

4 The debate in the UN: 1992–5

1 *The Independent*, 7 January 1992.
2 Status of Contributions as of 31 January 1992, UN Doc. ST/ADM/SER.B/371, 5 February 1992 and Report of the Secretary – General: Administrative and Budgetary Aspects of the Financing of the United Nations Peacekeeping Operations, UN Doc. A/47/484, 29 September 1992, Annexes I & II, pp. 4–13.
3 *Le Monde Dossiers et Documents*, no 211, Join 1993, p. 4.
4 Tenth Conference of Heads of State or Government of Non-Aligned Countries,

Jakarta, 1–6 September 1992, Final Document, para. 32 in UN Doc. NAC 10/Doc.11/Rev.1, 6 September 1992.

5 A/Res/47/62, adopted at the 84th plenary meeting of the General Assembly.

6 Question of Equitable Representation on and Increase in the Membership of the Security Council, *Report of the Secretary-General*, UN Doc.A/48/264 and Add. 1, Add. 2 and Add. 2/Corr. 1, Add. 3 and 4, 28 July 1993.

7 See UN Doc. GAOR, A/48/PV.61, 23 November 1993; see also UN Doc. GAOR, A/48/PV.62, 23 November 1993 and UN Doc. GAOR, A/48/PV.64, 24 November 1993.

8 Resolution 48/26 of 3 December 1993.

9 Question of Equitable Representation on and Increase in the Membership of the Security Council: Report of the Secretary-General, op. cit., p. 91.

10 Ibid., p. 41.

11 Ibid., p. 84.

12 Ibid., pp. 18–19.

13 Ibid., pp. 91–2.

14 For the views of Austria, Belgium, Ireland see UN Doc. A/49/965, 18 September 1995 and for Denmark, Finland and Sweden see UN Doc. A/AC.2475, 14 June 1995.

15 Question No H-856/95, by Mr Kranidiotis on the Representation of the European Union in the Security Council, in EU Doc. 95/389, 12 December 1995.

16 *The Independent*, 9 July 1993.

17 His statement is cited in E. Matanle, *The UN Security Council. Prospects for Reform*, Discussion Paper 62, London: Royal Institute of International Affairs, 1995, p. 30.

18 Remarks by Mr Fedotov, Permanent Representative of Russia to the UN, in the General Assembly, cited in UN Doc. GAOR, A/49/PV.32, 14 October 1994, p. 10.

19 Matanle, op. cit., p. 20.

20 For the Japanese stance on the issue see R. Drift, *Japan's Quest For a Permanent Security Council Seat: A Matter of Pride or Justice?*, London; Macmillan, 2000, pp. 174–9.

21 Statement by Ambassador Gerhard Henze, Acting Permanent Representative of Germany to the UN, in the Open-Ended Working Group, 17 May 1994, p. 4.

22 Question of Equitable Representation on and Increase in the Membership of the Security Council: Report of the Secretary-General, op. cit., p. 54.

23 Matanle, op. cit., pp. 21–2; see also Drift, op. cit., pp. 77–94; see also R. Drift, 'Japan and Security Council reform: Multilateralism at a turning point?', *Asian Pacific Law and Policy Journal*, vol. 14(1), 2000, p. 5.

24 Matanle, op. cit., p. 27.

25 See Roundtable on Security Council Reform, Online. Available HTTP: <http://www.ncrb.unac.org/unreform/roundtables/SCreform.html> (accessed 4 February 2003).

26 See the comments of J. Paul, 'Security Council reform: Arguments about the future of the United Nations system, February 1995, Online. Available HTTP: <http://www.globalpolicy.org/security/pubs/secref.htm> (accessed 6 January 2003).

27 More specifically, they had suggested the incorporation in the Council's Rules of Procedures of provisions for (i) the invitation of non-members of the Council to participate in the informal consultations, (ii) the conduct of substantive briefings by the President of the Security Council to the general membership promptly after each informal consultation of the whole, including information on draft resolutions, presidential statements and the views of the members of the Council on subject matters under consideration at such consultation;

(iii) informal consultations to be announced in advance in the *UN Journal* and (iv) the circulation of the agenda for informal consultations to all UN members. See Position paper of the Movement of Non-Aligned Countries, 13 February 1995, contained in UN Doc. A/AC.247/5(i), cluster II, found in UN Doc. A/49/965, 18 September 1995.

28 Ibid., cluster II, 2B; see also N. Reid, Informal Consultations, January 1999. Available online at: http://www.globalpolicyorg/security/informal/natalie.htm (accessed 10 January 2003).

29 To this effect, they had proposed the institutionalization of wide-ranging consultations of the Council with the non-members. These included efforts by the Council to consult more actively non-members of the Council involved in issues under consideration. Especially those states which would be affected by Council decisions should be invited to convey their opinions directly to it, comment on draft resolutions concerning the imposition of sanctions and the conduct of peacekeeping or enforcement operations. Consultations with non-permanent members should be extended to all subsidiary organs of the Council, such as the Sanctions Committees, the non-aligned states claimed. Finally, they urged the institutionalization of (i) regular briefings of the President of the Council to the general membership on issues before the Council and (ii) consultations between the President of the Council with respective Chairmen of the regional groups on important issues. See Position paper of the Movement of Non-Aligned Countries, op. cit., cluster II, 1B.

30 Ibid., cluster II, 1A.

31 For a detailed analysis of the measures that were adopted in this period see M. Wood, 'Security Council working methods and procedure: recent developments', *International and Comparative Law Quarterly*, 45(1), 1996, pp. 150–61; see also E. Luck, *Reforming the United Nations: Lessons from a History in Progress*, Academic Council on the United Nations System, International Relations Studies and the United Nations Occasional Papers, no 1, 2003, pp. 13–14; see also Decisions by the Security Council related to its working methods and procedures, 1993–present. Available online at: http://www.globalpolicyorg/security/reform/decision.htm (accessed 20 January 2003).

32 See, for instance, the views of Brazil, Nigeria, Pakistan, in UN Doc. S/PV.3483, 16 December 1994, pp. 5–6 and 9.

33 See Roundtable on Security Council Reform, op. cit.

34 Remarks by Mr Sardenberg, Permanent Representative of Brazil to the UN, in the Security Council, cited in UN Doc. S/PV.3483, 16 December 1994, p. 6.

35 Remarks by Mr Wibisono, Permanent Representative of Indonesia to the UN, in the Security Council, ibid., pp. 20–1.

36 Position paper of the Movement of Non-Aligned Countries, op. cit. See also B. Fassbender, *UN Security Council Reform and the Right of Veto. A Constitutional Perspective*, The Hague: Kluwer Law International, 1998, p. 248.

37 Remarks by Mr Jele, Permanent Representative of South Africa to the UN, in the General Assembly, cited in UN Doc. GAOR, A/50/PV.59, 14 November 1995, p. 7.

38 Remarks by Mr Abdelah, Permanent Representative of Tunisia to the UN, in the General Assembly, cited in UN Doc. GAOR, A/50/PV.58, 14 November 1995, p. 7.

39 Remarks by Mr Jele, op. cit.

40 In its statement in the Open-Ended Working Group in 1996, India said: 'Whatever the decision in regard either to keeping of the veto or elimination of the veto, or its curtailment or its regulation of use, my delegation firmly believes that there should be no discrimination between the present permanent members

and the new permanent members on this score'. See the statement of India cited in Fassbender, op. cit., p. 261.

41 Question of Equitable Representation on and Increase in the Membership of the Security Council: Report of the Secretary-General, op. cit., p. 48.

42 Ibid., p. 47.

43 Ibid., pp. 47–8.

44 Ibid., p. 48.

45 See UN Doc. A/AC.247/5 (f), found in UN Doc. A/49/965, 18 September 1995.

46 Equador, Guatemala, Nicaragua and Panama were members of the NAM.

47 Remarks by Mr Martinez Blanco, Permanent Representative of Honduras to the UN, in the General Assembly, cited in UN Doc. GAOR, A/50/PV.56, 13 November 1995, p. 14. The Representative of Honduras made explicitly clear that he was speaking on behalf of the Central American states.

48 The CARICOM states that belonged to the NAM were the following: Bahamas, Barbados, Belize, the Commonwealth of Dominica, Grenada, Guyana, Jamaica, Saint Lucia, Suriname and Trinidad and Tobago.

49 See UN Doc. GAOR, A/50/PV.56, 13 November 1995, p. 14; see also remarks by Mr Insaually, Permanent Representative of Guyanna to the UN, in the General Assembly, cited in UN Doc. GAOR, A/50/PV.58, 14 November 1995, pp. 1–3.

50 Ibid.

51 See *Reformes des Nations Unies: Position Africaine Commune*, OAU Doc. NY/OAU/POL/84/94/Rev. 2, 2 September 1994; see also the English version of the communique in UN Doc. A/AC.247/1996/CPR.6, 25 April 1996.

52 Remarks by Mr Jele, op. cit., pp. 6–7.

53 Remarks by Mr Lamptey, Permanent Representative of Ghana to the UN, in the General Assembly, cited in UN Doc. GAOR, A/50/PV.59, op. cit., pp. 17–18.

54 Remarks by Mr Etefa, Permanent Representative of Ethiopia to the UN, in the General Assembly, cited in UN Doc. GAOR, A/50/PV.60, 15 November 1995, pp. 7–8.

55 Remarks by Mr Kaabachi, Permanent Representative of Tunisia to the UN, in the General Assembly, cited in UN Doc. GAOR, A/53/PV.65, 20 November 1998, pp. 38–9.

56 Remarks by Mr Matiko, Permanent Representative of Tanzania to the UN, in the General Assembly, cited in UN Doc. GAOR, A/50/PV.60, 15 November 1995, pp. 4–5.

57 Remarks by Mr Kamunanwire, Permanent Representative of Uganda to the UN, in the General Assembly, cited in UN Doc. A/50/PV.56, 13 November 1995, p. 15.

58 Remarks by Mr Sengue, Permanent Representative of Zimbabwe to the UN, in the General Assembly, cited in UN Doc. GAOR, A/50/PV.59, op. cit., p. 3; see also UN Doc. GAOR, A/51/PV.45, 30 October 1996, pp. 13–14.

59 Remarks by Mr Muthaua, Permanent Representative of Kenya to the UN, in the General Assembly, cited in UN Doc. GAOR, A/50/PV.57, 13 November 1995, pp. 24–5.

60 Remarks by Mr Jele, Permanent Representative of South Africa to the UN, op. cit., p. 7.

61 Remarks by Mr Kamunanwire, op. cit., p. 15.

62 Jordan stuck to the position it had elaborated in 1993; see Question of Equitable Representation on and Increase in the Membership of the Security Council, *Report of the Secretary-General*, op. cit., p. 10.

63 See for instance the remarks by Mr Jele, op. cit., p. 7 and by Mr Muthaura, Permanent representative of Kenya to the UN, in the General Assembly, cited in UN Doc. GAOR, A/50/57, 13 November 1995, p. 24.

64 *Reformes Des Nations Unies: Position Africaine Commune*, op. cit.
65 See statement by Chile in Question of Equitable Representation on and Increase in the Membership of the Security Council, *Report of the Secretary-General*, op. cit., pp. 16–17.
66 Press Release GA/8599, 23 November 1993.
67 Press Release GA/8599, 23 November 1993. For the position of Egypt and Chile see Fassbender, op. cit., p. 256.
68 See, for instance, statement by Ambassador Kamal, Permanent Representative of Pakistan in the Open-Ended Working Group, 27 March 1996; see also Statement by Ambassador Londono-Paredes, the Permanent Representative of Colombia, in the Open-Ended Working Group, 28 March 1996.
69 Mexico was one of the few that adopted a diverse position regarding the particular number of new non-permanent seats. It presented a proposal that would have increased the size of the Council from 15 to 20 seats by creating five new non-permanent seats to be allocated as follows: one for Africa, one for Asia, one for Latin America and the Caribbean, one to alternate every two years between the Western European group and the Eastern European group, and one to alternate every two years between Germany and Japan. Since Mexico recognized that it was necessary to accept Germany and Japan on the Security Council, its proposal provided for the creation of a special rotating non-permanent seat for the two countries. For the proposal of Mexico see UN Doc. A/247/5 (h), April 1995, found in UN Doc. GAOR, A/49/47, op. cit.; see also remarks by Mr Tello, Permanent Representative of Mexico to the UN, in the General Assembly, cited in UN Doc. GAOR, A/50/PV.57, 13 November 1995, pp. 5–7.
70 See UN Press Release SG/8995, 14 November 1995, p. 7. See also intervention by the Permanent Representative of Pakistan to the UN in the Open-ended Working group on Security Council reform, 27 March 1996. Available online at: http://www.un.int/Pakistan/19960327.htm (accessed 8 May 2003).
71 Position paper of the Movement of Non-Aligned Countries, op. cit.
72 Ibid., cluster II.
73 For the common position of these states see UN Doc.A/AC.247/5 (c), 9 May 1995, found in UN Doc. A/49/965, 18 September 1995.
74 See the common position paper of the Nordic countries, in UN Doc. A/AC.247/5(j), 14 June 1995, found in UN Doc. A/49/965, 18 September 1995.
75 UN Doc. A/AC.247/1996/CRP.18, 3 July 1996; see also Fassbender, op. cit., p. 258.
76 For the Spanish position see Working Paper by Spain, Summary of Ideas on a Possible System of More Frequent Rotation in Additional Non-Permanent Seats in the Security Council, 28 February 1996, in UN Doc.A/AC.247/1996/CRP.10, 4 June 1996; details of the Spanish proposal can be also found in UN Doc. A/50/47/Add.1, annex VIII, 4 June 1996. See also remarks by Mr Yanez-Barnuero, Permanent Representative of Spain to the UN, in the General Assembly, in UN Doc. GAOR, A/50/57, 13 November 1995, pp. 8–9.
77 See Working Paper by Spain, op. cit.
78 See position paper of Turkey, in UN Doc. A/AC.247/5(I), found in UN Doc.A/49/965, 18 September 1995.
79 See the remarks of Paolo Fulci, Permanent Representative of Italy to the UN, in the General Assembly, cited in UN Doc. GAOR, A/50/PV.56, 13 November 1995, p. 16.
80 Ibid.
81 Ibid.
82 Ibid., pp. 16–18; see also remarks by Ambassador Paolo Fulci on Equitable Representation in the Open-Ended Working Group, 22 April 1996.

83 The reform proposal of Italy is contained in UN Doc. A/AC.274/5 (g), annex, 15 May 1995, found in UN Doc. A/49/965, 18 September 1995. For further details about the Italian position see Italy and the reform of the UN Security Council. Available online at: http://www.italyemb.org/SecurityCouncil.htm (accessed 5 July 2003). In this site one can find a revised proposal for an enlargement of the Security Council submitted by Italy to the Open-Ended Working group on Council reform in 1997.

84 Ibid. See also Statement by Ambassador Francesco Fulci, the Permanent Representative of Italy to the UN, in the General Assembly, 29 October 1996.

85 M. Pedrazzi, 'Italy's Approach to UN Security Council Reform', *International Spectator*, July–September 2000, p. 55.

86 See the reform proposal of Italy in UN Doc. A/AC.274/5 (g), 15 May 1995, appendix II.

87 Roundtable on Security Council reform, op. cit.

88 Ibid., p. 8.

89 For the position of Canada see UN Doc.A/50/PV.57, 13 November 1995, pp. 7–8.

90 Remarks by Mr Elaraby, Permanent Representative of Egypt to the UN, in the General Assembly, cited in UN Doc. GAOR, A/50/PV.58, op. cit., p. 14.

91 UN Doc. GAOR, A/51/PV.45, 30 October 1996, p. 10.

92 UN Doc. GAOR, A/50/PV.57, 13 November 1995, p. 11.

93 Remarks by Mr Guardigli, Permanent Representative of San Marino to the UN, in the General Assembly, cited in UN Doc. UN Doc. GAOR, A/50/PV.58, op. cit., p. 8.

94 Remarks by Mr Park, Permanent Representative of the Republic of Korea to the UN, in the General Assembly, cited in UN Doc. GAOR, A/51/PV.45, op. cit., p. 9.

95 UN Doc. GAOR, A/50/PV.59, 14 November 1995, p. 21.

96 See Spain's ideas on Security Council reform. Available online at: http://www.globalpolicy.org/security/reform/spain.htm (accessed 15 February 2003).

97 See remarks by Mr Celem, Permanent Representative of Turkey to the UN, in the General Assembly, cited in UN Doc. GAOR, A/51/PV.45, op. cit., p. 12.

5 The debate in the UN: 1996–2000

1 See UN Doc.A/50/47, para. 26 and UN Doc.A/51/PV.45, 30 October 1996, p. 11.

2 B. Russett *et al.*, 'Breaking the restructuring logjam', in B. Russett (ed.), *The Once and the Future Security Council*, London: Macmillan, 1997, p. 158.

3 See speech by Mr Gorelik, Permanent Representative of Russia to the UN, in the General Assembly, cited in UN Doc. GAOR, A/52/PV.64, 5 December 1997, p. 11 and in UN Doc. GAOR, A/51/PV.45, 30 October 1996, pp. 19–20.

4 Bill Richardson, the American chief diplomat in the UN, stated that 'we have no flexibility above and beyond 20–21 seats on a reformed Council. This would permit expansion of the Council by one-third, with up to five new permanent members'; see statement on Security Council reform made by B. Richardson, Permanent Representative of the United States to the UN, in the Open-Ended Working Group, 17 July 1997.

5 Statement to the General Assembly by Sergey Lavrov, cited in UN Doc. GAOR A/53/PV.63, 19 November 1998, p. 23; see also the remarks of Mr Fedotov, the Russian Permanent Representative to the UN, in the General Assembly in UN Doc. GAOR, A/50/PV.60. 15 November 1995, p. 4.

6 See speech by Mr Dejammet, Permanent Representative of France to the UN, in the General Assembly, cited in UN Doc. GAOR, A/52/PV.64, 5 December 1997, p. 15.

7 See the remarks of Mr Xuexian, Permanent Representative of China to the UN, in the General Assembly, cited in UN Doc. A/51/45, 30 October 1996, pp. 17–18.

8 For the position of China regarding the veto see Statement on the Veto by Ambassador Sh. Guofang, Deputy Permanent Representative of China to the UN, in the Open-Ended Working Group, 23 April 1998. For the position of France see the remarks of Mr Ladsous, Permanent Representative of France to the UN, in the General Assembly in UN Doc. GAOR, A/50/PV.57, 13 November 1995, p. 18.

9 Statement by Ambassador K. Inderfurth, US Representative for Special Political Affairs, in the Open-Ended Working Group, 27 March 1996; see also statement by the spokesman of the Department of State, 18 July 1997, Daily Briefing No 109 and the statement by R. Skiar, US Representative to the UN for UN Reform and Management, in the Open-Ended Working Group, 24 March 1999.

10 Statement by Sir J. Weston, KCMG, Permanent Representative of United Kingdom of Great Britain and Northern Ireland to the UN, in the Open-Ended Working Group, 21 May 1996.

11 Statement by S. Lavrov in the Open-Ended Working Group of the General Assembly on Security Council Reform, 29 May 1998.

12 Statement by S. Lavrov in the Open-Ended Working Group of the General Assembly on Security Council Reform, 22 May 1996; see also similar statements which were made by Lavrov in 29 May and 19 November 1998 and the speech of Mr Gorelik in the General Assembly, cited in UN Doc. GAOR, A/51/PV.45, 30 October 1996, p. 20.

13 See for instance the Russian position in UN Doc. GAOR, A/42/PV.64, 5 December 1997.

14 By linking the debate on the future status of Germany and Japan in the Security Council with the developing states' desiderata, the permanent members managed to pass part of the buck for the prevention of Bonn and Tokyo from joining with full rights the most exclusive club of the world to the states of NAM. On the notion of buck-passing see Th. Christensen and J. Snyder, 'Chain-gangs and passed bucks: predicting alliance patterns in multipolarity', *International Organization*, 44(2), 1990, pp. 137–68.

15 *Asahi Shimbum* (newspaper), 31 January 1998.

16 For the text of the Razali Plan see Appendix 3; for an analysis of the Razali reform plan see R. Drifte, *Japan's Quest for a Permanent Security Council Seat. A Matter of Pride or Justice?*, Basingstoke: Macmillan, 2000, pp. 181–5; see also D. Bourantonis and K. Magliveras, The enlargement of the UN Security Council: reflections from the current debate', *Politics*, 22 (1), 2002, pp. 24–30.

17 Cited in B. Fassbender, *UN Security Council Reform and the Right of Veto. A Constitutional Perspective*, Hague: Kluwer, 1998, p. 270.

18 Statement by Ambassador B. Richardson, Permanent Representative of the United States to the UN, in the Open-Ended Working Group on Council reform, 17 July 1997.

19 See speech by Mr Dejammet, Permanent Representative of France to the UN, in the General Assembly, in UN Doc.A/52/PV.64, 5 December 1997, p. 16.

20 Ibid.

21 See letter by the Permanent Representative of Germany to the United Nations, Ambassador T. Eitel, to all Permanent Representatives, 20 March 1997.

22 See the Communique of the Meeting of Ministers for Foreign Affairs and Heads of Delegation of the Movement of Non-Aligned Countries at New York, 25 September 1997, para. 15; see also the Final Document of the XII Minister-

ial Conference of the Movement of Non-Aligned Countries, New Delhi, 7–8 April 1997, para. 28.

23 Ibid.

24 Statement by the Permanent Representative of Pakistan to the UN, in the Open-Ended Working Group on Council Reform, 20 April 1997.

25 See speech by Mr Ahmad, Permanent Representative of Pakistan to the UN, in the General Assembly, cited in UN Doc. GAOR, A/51/PV.63, 4 December 1997, p. 12.

26 E. Mattanle, *The UN Security Council. Prospects for Reform*, Discussion Paper 62, London: The Royal Institute of International Affairs, 1995, p. 18.

27 Speech by Mr Wibisono, Permanent Representative of Indonesia to the UN, in the General Assembly, cited in UN Doc. GAOR, A/53/PV.64, 20 November 1998, p. 10.

28 Speech by Mr Elaraby, Permanent Representative of Egypt to the UN, in the General Assembly, cited in UN Doc. GAOR, A/53/PV.63, 19 November 1998, p. 2; Similarly, Pakistan wondered '[h]ow great countries, which pride themselves on being the new realities in a world half a century down the line, could probably entertain the ambition to have their new status recognized on the basis of a vote which could perhaps be even less than a half of the total membership of the United Nations'; for the position of Pakistan see UN Doc. GAOR, A/53/PV.65, 20 November 1998.

29 P. Fulci, 'Italy and the reform of the UN Security Council', *International Spectator*, XXXIV, 1999, p. 13.

30 Ibid.

31 Ibid.

32 See the statement by Ambassador P. Fulci of Italy in the Open-Ended Working Group on Security Council Reform, 23 June 1998. He stated that: 'the strategy of the pretenders is clear. They want to foster a piecemeal approach to the Council's reforms such as having a framework resolution adopted by a minority of member states, in the hope that later on, others will jump on the bandwagon to give them the additional votes needed for the formal amendments to the Charter'.

33 Speech by Mr Fulci in the General Assembly, cited in UN Doc. GAOR, A/53/PV.66, 23 November 1998, p. 5.

34 Fulci, 'Italy and the reform of the UN Security Council', op. cit., p. 13.

35 For the text of the draft resolution see UN Doc. A/52/L.7, 22 October 1997.

36 Letter by Mr Owada, Permanent Representative of Japan to the United Nations, to all Permanent Representatives, 23 October 1997; the main text of the letter is cited in Drifte, op. cit., p. 184.

37 Letter by Ambassador T. Eitel, Permanent Representative of Germany to the UN, to all Permanent Representatives, 24 October 1997; see also Drifte, op. cit., p. 185.

38 Fulci, 'Italy and the reform of the UN Security Council', op. cit., p. 13.

39 Draft Resolution A/53/L.16 of 28 October 1998 was sponsored by the following states: Afghanistan, Argentina, Canada, Colombia, Egypt, Equatorial Guinea, Fiji, Gambia, Indonesia, Italy, Lebanon, Malta, Mexico, New Zealand, Pakistan, Papua New Guinea, Qatar, Republic of Korea, San Marino, Sierra Leone, Singapore, Solomon Islands, Spain, Swaziland, Syria, Turkey and Zimbabwe.

40 See paragraph 65 of the Final Document issued by the Heads of State or Government of the Movement of Non-Aligned States, at their summit held in Durban (South Africa), from 29 August to 3 September 1998.

41 See UN Doc. GAOR, A/54/PV.63, and the speech of Mr Young, Permanent Representative of the Republic of Korea to the UN, in the General Assembly, cited in UN Doc. GAOR, A/53/PV.65, p. 22.

42 Speech by Mr Adam, Permanent Representative of Belgium to the UN, in the General Assembly, cited in UN Doc. GAOR, A/53/PV.64, 20 November 1998, p. 29.

43 See draft resolution A/53/L.42 of 18 November 1998: Amendments to draft resolution A/53/L.16. It was sponsored by Australia, Austria, Brazil, Bulgaria, the Czech Republic, Denmark, Estonia, France, Germany, Hungary, Ireland, Japan, Luxembourg, the Netherlands, Poland, Portugal, Britain and the United States.

44 See for instance the remarks made by the German representative in the UN stating that 'we have the impression that the sponsors of A/53/L.16 always want to preclude serious discussion on something which does not yet exist', in UN Doc. GAOR, A/53/PV.64, 20 November 1998, p. 19; see also the remarks made by the British representative in the UN who said that 'contrary to ill-founded rumour, it has never been our intention to table a hasty resolution', in UN Doc. GAOR A/53/PV.65, 20 November 1998, p. 33. Similar statements were made by Japan and France (found in UN Doc. GAOR, A/53/PV.65, 20 November 1998, p. 14 and pp. 37–8) and the United States (found in UN Doc. GAOR, A/53/PV.66, 23 November 1998, p. 9).

45 See the speech made by the British representative to the UN, in the General Assembly, cited in UN Doc A/53/PV.65, 20 November 1998, p. 34.

46 For the views of Russia see the remarks by S. Lavrov in the General Assembly, cited in UN Doc. GAOR, A/53/PV.63, 19 November 1998, pp. 22–4. For the views of China see the remarks by Mr Sh. Guofang, Permanent Representative of China to the UN, in the General Assembly, cited in UN Doc. GAOR, A/53/PV.64, 20 November 1998, pp. 5–7.

47 The 36 sponsors of draft resolution A/53/L.16/Rev.1 (a version of draft resolution A/53/L.16) were the following: Afghanistan, Argentina, Canada, Chad, China, Colombia, Democratic Republic of the Congo, Egypt, Equatorial Guinea, Fiji, Gambia, Indonesia, Iran, Italy, Lebanon, Libya, Malta, Mexico, New Zealand, Pakistan, Panama, Papua New Guinea, Qatar, Republic of Korea, Russia, Samoa, San Marino, Sierra Leone, Singapore, Solomon Islands, Spain, Swaziland, Syria, Turkey and Zimbabwe.

48 For the text of the resolution see UN Doc. A/RES/53/30, 1 December 1998. Resolution 53/30 was adopted at the 66th plenary meeting of the General Assembly on 23 November 1998.

Index

Printed in the United Kingdom
by Lightning Source UK Ltd.
133198UK00001B/11/A